# Real Players?
## drama, technology and education

# Real Players?
## drama, technology and education

*John Carroll, Michael Anderson*
*and David Cameron*

**Trentham Books**

Stoke on Trent, UK and Sterling, USA

**Trentham Books Limited**

| | |
|---|---|
| Westview House | 22883 Quicksilver Drive |
| 734 London Road | Sterling |
| Oakhill | VA 20166-2012 |
| Stoke on Trent | USA |
| Staffordshire | |
| England ST4 5NP | |

First published 2006

**British Library Cataloguing-in-Publication Data**
A catalogue record for this book is available from the
British Library

ISBN-10: 1-85856-365-8
ISBN-13: 978-1-85856-365-7

Cover shows a scene from *Perfect* at Contact Theatre,
Manchester.

Figures 4.1 and 4.2 are from Blast Theory's *Uncle Roy
All Around You*, a collaboration with the Mixed Reality
Lab at University of Nottingham and supported by an
Arts and Humanities Research Board Innovation Award,
Equator, BT, Microsoft Research and Arts Council
England with Lottery Funds. These images are
© Blast Theory.

Designed and typeset by Trentham Print Design Ltd,
Chester and printed in Great Britain by Hobbs the
Printers Ltd, Hampshire.

# Contents

# Acknowledgements

We thank Trentham for their patient support of this book and in particular Gillian Klein for steering the work through to publication.

Some of the chapters of this book have evolved from papers published in other places. We would also like to thank and acknowledge the publishers of our earlier work reprised and revised in this book. They include:

Anderson, M (2004) 'Drama Futures: Possibilities for Research, Advocacy and Policy in the 21st Century', *NJ: The National Journal of Drama Australia*, 28(2), pp31-41

Anderson, M (2005) 'New Stages: Challenges for Teaching the Aesthetics of Drama Online', *Journal of Aesthetic Education*, 39(2), pp2-12

Cameron, D (2005) *The Net Generation goes to University?*, Proceedings of the Journalism Education Association conference, Surfers Paradise

Cameron, D and Carroll, J (2004) 'The Story So Far... The Researcher as a Player in Games Analysis', *Media International Australia: Games and Gaming*, 10th February, 1, p68

Carroll, J (2002) 'The Theatre of Surveillance: Invisible Theatre for Invisible Audiences', in B Rasmussen and A-L Ostern (eds) *Playing Betwixt and Between: The Idea Dialogues 2001*, Bergen: IDEA, pp203-208

Carroll, J (2002) 'Digital drama: A Snapshot of Evolving Forms', *Drama and Learning: Melbourne Studies in Education*, November, 43(2), pp130-141

Carroll, J (2004) 'Digital Interactive Drama and Process Drama', *Drama Research*, 3, Gateshead, UK: National Drama publications, pp89-99

Carroll, J (2004) 'Digital Pre-text: Process Drama and Everyday Technology' in C Hatton and M Anderson, *State of Our Art: NSW Perspectives in Educational Drama*, Sydney: Currency Press, pp66-77

Carroll, J (2005) 'Digital Natives and Virtual Literacy: Process Drama and On-line Learning', *International Journal of Learning*, 11, Havana, Cuba: Proceedings of The Eleventh International Literacy and Education Research Network Conference, 2004, pp1211-1217

Carroll, J (2005) 'YTLKIN2ME? Drama in the Age of Digital Reproduction', *NJ Drama Australia Journal*, 29(1) and *IDEA Journal*, 3, pp15-23

Carroll, J and Cameron, D (2003) 'To the Spice Islands': Interactive Process Drama', Proceedings of the DAC conference 2003, published by the Fine Art Forum, retrieved January 2006, from www.fineartforum.org

Carroll J, and Cameron, D (2005) 'Playing the Game: Role Distance and Digital Performance', *IDEA/Applied Theatre Research Journal*, 6

## Dedication

*This book would not be possible without the innovative work of Dorothy Heathcote. Her practice, teaching and art remain an inspiration to teachers everywhere who care about making education relevant to the lives of young people.*

# Foreword

In July 1993 I listened to John Carroll speak at an international drama conference of teachers who had gathered to celebrate the housing of a computer based archive of my work in an English university. He spoke of the coming impact of e-mail and the Internet as technological forces to be considered by schools and teachers.

I remember thinking at the time, 'so long as they don't just tack it on to the long list of subjects to be learned about and be instructed and examined in.' Then I filed it away with that baggage of memory stuff students are expected to want to get interested in, as if schools are the only sources of learning. Well, these things – mobile phones, text messages, digital cameras and home videos – escaped the dead hand of schools and entered the real world of systemic change. While formal learning establishments hang on to earlier (and once very useful and essential) modes of teaching students, our youngsters are outpacing my generation and that of most teachers since my heyday. I'm glad to recognise from the text you are about to read that I am a 'digital immigrant'. That places me nicely in a relationship with the younger 'digital natives'[1], including my granddaughter aged 5 who is handling the mouse on her mother's computer with that coordination of hand, eye and sound demanded by the images she processes with such profound pertinacious persistency. Sorry, as a grandmother I couldn't resist that last bit! Unfortunately though, her school timetable follows in the main, the old model. Time divided by subjects divided by tests.

Perhaps the digital natives will cause some of the established walls to weaken? I saw it happen in Northumberland when designing the garden for the new NHS hospital along with nine brave teachers and thirty-five fifteen-year old volunteers. The relationship demanded that the following pedagogical walls were *voluntarily disallowed*:

- Teachers hold the knowledge to be learned
- Teachers keep a grip on the order in which students encounter content during the learning process
- Students will abandon any awkward challenging questions
- Students will leave their complex, dense muddled ideas about hospitals, gardens, illness, death and birth outside the school where they belong
- Students will remember that teachers know more than they do.

We had to label these walls in order to remember to forget them, and most of the time it worked to the good of all of us including the hospital garden. We got rid of the 'dummy-run'[2] syndrome, a term which John introduced me to years ago. A more process-based approach permitted us to use drama systems as a universal joint for all the angles we explored. There's a good technical image I learned from being married to an engineer who dreamed up possibilities much as teachers do, to enable learning rather than instruction. Bruner, in one of his throwaway remarks, spoke of drama as being 'a safe *arena*' (note the active, constrained focused term) 'in which children could do things experimentally without the due consequences encountered in the outside world'. I'm also grateful to a colleague of mine, who speaking as a philosopher during a school drama session, remarked that '...school is far from safe but the drama class may be'.

Now if the digital immigrants will be humble and astute enough to let the digital natives into the arena of needing information and exploring how to process it, maybe some shift may come about in considering what schools are for, with a move towards a more systemic mode of engaging students and staff in cooperative learning. John Humphrys, the intrepid news interviewer on BBC Radio 4, asked in his book *The Devil's Advocate* (2000) What can we know? What ought we to do? And what can we hope for? These questions seem to me to be particularly pertinent when considering the ideas in this book. The writers place the two seemingly dissonant notions of drama and technology in close proximity and consider how a synthesis might benefit the pattern of future schooling by drawing on the reality of student life experiences.

On the face of it drama emphasises human relationships explored by groups in active participation during immediate time – what Shakespeare has called 'holding the mirror up to nature'. Its many manifestations are well recorded and preserved as well as being freshly worked upon by succeeding generations seeking to find contemporary meanings from older human matters of concern. It seems ludicrous to associate this well tried art form with the complex technology so domestically expressed by small humans talking to each other across space and air holding tiny instruments and pecking at digits with eloquent fingers and thumbs while they stride over pavements and busy roads demanding close coordination of hand, eye and balance. The common ground is human interaction and summoning of imperative point of view in the participants. The differences are only in the outward show. I am aware that I am being overly simplistic, but then I'm not writing the book; you the reader will have to embrace the possibility of such a symbiosis as you follow the authors.

Now, I am part of the way on this journey not because I can remotely visualise how the technology actually works, any more than I comprehend how John Humphrys and I encounter each other through my radio each morning. What I do know is that our minds meet because I know how to turn the switch to bring about the encounter, and I have to believe it will be worth the effort.

I had the good fortune recently to be involved in a close encounter of symbiosis between literature, theatre and technology which convinces me that the basic elements of drama – ancient and proven shape shifter as it is – naturally can embrace close encounter with the technological advances in communication systems which will have changed and modified in the time it is taking me to write these ideas on the paper. Technology is the symbiotic shape shifter of our age.

I was given the brief by the education director of Birmingham Repertory Theatre of helping local teachers of English and drama to devise ways of interesting high school students in Bram Stoker's Victorian novel *Dracula*. The theatre was mounting a production and had commissioned a new script. *Dracula* is not a book which attracts me, with its vampire associations and images of fangs and marks of teeth on female necks. However it was a challenge to see how such seemingly outmoded material might be made attractive to modern students. It is easy to find amusement in the naïve blood transfusions, the efficacy of garlic as a protection against evil and the power of Dracula himself to shape shift into dogs and hide away in graveyards during daylight.

Bram Stoker proved to have a remarkable skill, born no doubt of his close interest in theatre and friendship with Henry Irving. His writing moves smoothly between descriptions of places and events and the immediacy of dramatic dialogue between people. He marries literary and dramatic forms seamlessly on the pages so the reader is constantly lured between the two points of view of *seeing* there and *being* there. Furthermore, he presents every situation to the reader through communication lenses, the systems available at the time of Stoker's writing. The whole novel is presented and the story unfolds because the reader must accept the variety of forms available at the time. We encounter diaries, letters, phonographic recordings – the early wax discs – journals and telegrams. Stoker warns the reader '...all needless matters have been eliminated so that a history almost at variance with the possibilities of latter day belief may stand forth as simple fact...' All the records chosen are exactly contemporary with the text, the information given from the standpoint and within the range and knowledge of those who made them. Thus he causes the reader to switch points of view and vary what can be envisioned from multiple perspectives.

With hindsight I now realise that this is one of the richnesses which technology brings to the 'reader' – an amazing variety of systems for presenting information, which can be processed for a range of purposes. I see this happening in my small local library when I search for books and move around the computers being searched by people of a variety of ages and with a variety of purposes in mind.

Because as yet I had no new theatre text to rely on I concentrated on Stoker's range and the variety of 'voices' he presented me with in order to comprehend his intention regarding the surprisingly moral tale he engaged me in. I had just sorted all this out when the new script was delivered, and to my delight I found the modern author was presenting Stoker's book in theatre form through the symbiosis of modern technology and live actors. When I saw the play in performance I met computers, e-mails, mobile phone voice and text messages in exact mirroring of those Victorian systems Stoker used in his book on screen, all around me in voice and image and actors speaking dialogue as they always have in theatre, live and moving. The whole experience seamlessly drawing upon a blend of actuality and virtuality. I am convinced of the symbiotic possibilities between ancient art and contemporary artifice.

Could it happen in schooling? What has to change so that students are valued because they bring through the portals all their interests and energies and questions and muddled aspirations? First we digital immigrants have to welcome in the digital natives and provide materials for interrogation which release possibilities of working alongside one another. We can offer longer experience of human interaction. We can ease the way into school and community issues being moored alongside each other. We can bring the working world of resources, and getting and spending money and making and sustaining relationships and rearing children, and looking after the world in all its manifestations into the relative safety of schooling, where mistakes and errors are seen as productive, not shaming.

The big shift is to move from holding the information and doling it out like charity, to creating the circumstances where it is imperative to inquire, search out and interrogate the information we locate. If at present it isn't possible to merge the work of adults and the work of students because we don't value the contribution young children can bring to cultural development of the world's good, we can rely on proven drama systems to create 'the mirror to nature' and harness, through identification and empathy, the life knowledge which children will bring generously to meet us half way. The book which follows surely points us along the way.

*Dorothy Heathcote*
31 December, 2005

## Notes

1 Digital *Natives* (Prensky, 2001b) is a cultural/linguistic metaphor describing an innate comfort with digital technologies. It does not, and is not meant to relate to the potentially pejorative geographical applications of the term.

2 Dummy Run – a characteristic of transmission pedagogy that encourages student's passive participation in a learning situation. All student work is presented only to the teacher for assessment and judging. From Carroll, J. (1982) Growing Language, *NADIE Journal* vol. 7(2) pp 59-62.

# Introduction

avid Cameron was walking through a university computer laboratory recently. New students, younger than the first iteration of the Macintosh computers they were working on, sat surfing the Web, preparing digital presentations for class, and editing video with casual ease. Well, mostly. Somewhere, from up the back of the room, came the frustrated refrain of 'I hate computers'. A handful of students nodded in silent agreement.

Encountering that attitude can be confusing these days, because it's so easy to assume that all young people are digital media *savants*. New technology is supposed to be the domain of the next generation, who will see technology not for what it is (complex gadgets) but for what it allows them to do (live a certain lifestyle). Generation gaps have probably existed since young cave men and women started hanging around the waterhole with the wrong sort of crowd and experimenting with new forms of ochre body art. But the rapid flood of digital technology into so many aspects of our daily lives gives the current perceived generational divide a peculiar kind of plasticity. Sometimes the chasm is so great, young people seem to have a complex, almost alien, symbiotic relationship with technology. At other times ... well, count the number of middle-aged commuters who wear their iPods as a digital merit badge.

Regardless of age we are all, in the western world at least, surrounded by digital technology. Today's generation gap is less about ideological or demographic differences and more about demonstrated comfort and ability with the tools of everyday living. If you 'get it', as most young people seem to, you have the edge on those who use the same technology but in a less intuitive or instinctive way. We talk more about this generational difference throughout the book.

You may think a book like this would invite you to embrace technology in drama teaching and learning. Our approach to the digital world is simple. Students in drama classes today have been born into that digital world, whilst most of their teachers are still coming to terms with the changes in technology and their students' understanding of it. Young people generally do not see the Internet, DVDs or mobile telephones as technology, just as their teachers did not question the existence of telephones, radio and possibly television during their own childhood.

More importantly, at the heart of everything we do in teaching drama and making theatre is physical embodiment and live performance. Although interested in putting some arguments for the integration of drama and technology, we are not evangelists or technological determinists. We strongly believe that if digital technology does not make the drama experience for students more effective or the theatre experience for audiences more engaging, it is not worth having. Effective drama can still happen in an empty space with no modern digital technology.

Our commitment to the live form is at the core of teaching and performance but technology often can and does enrich and extend the imagination of our students. By technology we mean recent technology that includes video, the Internet, CD and DVD, mobile phones and PDAs. We refer to culture and its products as being 'mediatised', meaning that culture is now saturated with messages and images that are created through media of one kind or another, be it television, advertising or theatre itself. This mediation can transform drama if we engage with it for learning and other purposes.

Mediated performance, digital pretexts and video offer teachers and students the possibility of extending the experiences they already have in drama into new digital spaces. These spaces are not in opposition to the embodied (real) and traditional drama and theatre approach but are a natural partner to what drama educators do on a daily basis. We recognise that for many readers there is a tension between the real and the mediatised and between the live and the recorded. We can see it on the cover of this book, with the mediatised image and the live performer competing for the audience's attention. Although we understand this tension, if we allow the mediatised and the live to become a dichotomy we are in danger of losing our young students/audiences as they seek relevant performance forms in the mediatised world they have been born into.

The 'digital natives' (Prensky, 2001b) in classrooms and theatre spaces are demanding a different approach to learning. Drama education has been engaged in this discussion from early on because drama educators value the power of imagination, the central place of the child in learning and the importance of connecting with the audience in the theatre. We have an unparalleled opportunity to engage with the technology in upholding what is central to drama education and theatrical aesthetic – the understanding of the human condition and the power of imagination in the creation of art. Everything we say here is working towards supporting those aims and the central, essential element of drama and theatre: the live interaction between players, be they teachers, students, actors or audience. We argue that all are 'real players' – they just choose different stages on which to enact their drama.

Chapter 1 of this book considers how drama is changing and being changed in response to technology. Beyond the hype of technological determinists and short-sighted education management, technology can be a powerful tool for creation in drama. We discuss how mediated technology, process drama, performance and games become situated role, liveness and simulation. This leads us to consider the creative potential of mediated learning communities.

Chapter 2 looks at how drama is being transformed by technology. The history of technology is not as new as might be thought. After noting the antecedents of drama and technology that date from the early 20th Century, we consider the changes occurring in the dramatic aesthetic, often driven by the changed expectations of the digital natives in audiences and classrooms. We then examine how these changes are currently being demonstrated in schools, on stages and through the Internet.

This book is concerned with the ways young people in drama understand and interact with the art form in the midst of the digital revolution. Chapter 3 considers who these young people are and their expectations of learning and performance. How have schools, teachers and others responded to the challenges of students who have an unprecedented understanding and usage of technology? How can drama educators connect with these students to use technology as a powerful creative force in their classrooms? How might teachers use the aesthetics of drama education to take account of the online world?

Chapter 4 and Chapter 5 explore how Theatre For Young People (TYP) and Theatre in Education (TIE) have responded to the change in their audiences. We discuss some of the myths that relate to mediated performance and young people, and the way performance is changing through use of a more integrated approach to technology. Companies such as Contact in Manchester, Arena in Melbourne and C&T in Worcester provide examples of how TIE is being influenced and changed in response to audiences' demands. They use radically new approaches to the process of theatre devising, integrating digital performance technologies into the collaborative devising process. Chapter 5 considers how this has led to the concept of dramatic property.

Chapter 6 provides case studies of how situated role can be used in drama learning. The *To The Spice Islands* project and *Flood* were created by the authors using traditional drama approaches transformed by everyday technologies. The *To The Spice Islands* project recreated events surrounding a 1629 shipwreck for Dutch students through simple and accessible technologies and the use of process drama approaches including pretext. *Flood* was an applied theatre project used in the training of journalism students. The students were enrolled as reporters responding to the unfolding emergency of a flood in an Australian country town. This project used drama approaches linked with Web sites, including free and accessible artificial intelligence software, to create an authentic learning experience for these students.

Screen drama provides an exciting and creatively satisfying way for students to transcode their live drama experiences. Chapter 7 examines how screen performance has changed the way educators and others approach drama and discusses how the form has changed with the emergence in recent times of the reality and surveillance genres of television. How might drama educators and others use conventions such as role protection to create video drama that respects and protects young people?

Video games are another pervasive and influential medium. There has been recent interest in the ways the successful learning systems present in some video games might be harnessed by educators to support, enhance or transform classroom learning. Chapter 8 examines how the conventions of video games reflect many of the conventions of drama.

The research in the area of drama, education and technology is in its infancy. Chapter 9 discusses the issues relating to research in the area and provides three perspectives drawn from the authors' research experiences. Michael Anderson discusses the questions arising in the area and suggests methodologies to address them. John Carroll presents his research experience in creating mediated performances that examine the preferences of digital native audiences. David Cameron examines the evolving world of video games research and discusses its development for learning.

The book concludes with a series of observations about what we think the future might hold for drama education. Young people's involvement with technology is reviewed and we consider what education might be like in the future, knowing any image of the shape shifter that is technology is bound to be no more than a glimpse.

# 1

# Technology and the transformation of drama and learning

For better and for worse, the virtual world and the physical world are becoming very intermingled, they're no longer the separate places that they used to be. (Howard Rheingold[1], 2004)

## Adventures in time and space

A few years ago, we built a time machine.

You won't have heard about it in the news, or read about it in the science journals, but this amazing device took us back through time to the early hours of 4 June 1629.

Our destination was a magnificent sailing ship, the peak example of nautical technology and shipbuilders' art of her day. The Dutch East Indiaman *Batavia* was making her way through southern waters previously crossed by only a handful of European vessels. Nearing the end of her maiden voyage, *Batavia* had seven months of fairly uneventful sailing from Amsterdam behind her, and another month at sea before she reached her destination in Java. Yet despite the relatively smooth passage, she had been home to simmering tensions, intrigue and mutinous feuds among some of her passengers and crew.

Our history books tell us that some time after 3am *Batavia* would smash onto a coral reef off the West Australian coast.[2] We knew that a terrible legend of survival against the elements and a band of murderous mutineers was about to unfold. More than 300 men, women and children were in grave peril.

Our time machine might allow us to transmit messages to the passengers and crew of the ill-fated *Batavia*. In particular, we were concerned about the fate of a 10 year old girl called Wilhelmina, whose letters to home we had found in a musty museum archive three centuries later. Should we try to warn her of the awful danger lurking in the dark ocean ahead?

For the group of Dutch primary school students in our history class, the answer was clear[3]:

> Wilhelmina!!
> This is a warning from the future. You will be shipwrecked, try to prevent this and try to get off that ship.
> Dian, Bart, Jolanda and Marco.

> Wilhelmina
> There may be a mutiny coming.
> Your ship will lie on the bottom of the sea.
> Be prepared for it.
> Tell the captain.
> Take care,
> Joost, Anita, Arjen, Fenna and Patrick.

This was the beginning of our classroom adventures with the *Batavia*, detailed further in Chapter 6. Our remarkable time machine was built using free Web-based journal software (a blog). Our journey was powered by the imagination of students and teachers, and guided by drama in education principles, especially role-based process drama (O'Neill, 1995).

## Exploring digital worlds

Our imaginary voyage with the *Batavia* also marked the start of our journey towards this book. It was prompted by a desire to explore the potential of the world of digital technology as a context for drama, a place where art and science can merge almost seamlessly to create new worlds and engaging spaces for learning. And while much had already been written about both process drama and the dramatic forms emerging from digital technology, little had been said about the obvious connections and parallels that exist for learning.

Howard Rheingold observes that for most students in schools in the west, the relationship between the material world and the virtual world has never been more fluid. For the young Dutch students the fate of a girl of their own age in an impending shipwreck, despite being separated by time and space of 373 years and twelve thousand kilometres, was an authentic experience, even though it was framed dramatically within a process drama class. What gave it 'authenticity' (Bolton, 1998, p244) was a rigorous attention and respect for what was historically true: true for the scientist, the scholar, the artist. This focus on the authenticity and integrity of experiences, both real and virtual, connects the seemingly disparate areas of dramatic art and technological science.

## Real players

We use the term 'real players' to signify how technology and media are transforming traditional dramatic forms. Aspects of traditional learning communities are being changed when they engage with technology to create what might be called *mediated* learning communities.

Throughout the book we examine how this process operates with three key dramatic forms. Process drama can be transformed and enhanced with technology and media to create a new hybrid form, which we call *situated role*. This dramatically framed position shares all the features of process drama (O'Neill, 1995, p20) but is situated in a dramatically mediated 'reality' that augments the imagined context in a classroom. Adopting this framing could bring educators closer to the aims of Heathcote's Commission Model and other methods of situated learning. In this context, real players means drawing on students' real life experiences, while using technology to enhance dramatic role identities beyond the classroom and into real world communities of practice.

Secondly, technology and media are transforming traditional live performance to create a new sense of 'liveness' (Auslander, 1999) permeating popular culture. Used in this sense, 'real players' picks up on the irony of a culture that sees live performance as requiring technological augmentation, from the ubiquitous electric guitar to amplify music to the intimate video shots of performers played on vast screens placed next to arena stages at rock concerts.

Thirdly, the use of the term shows how traditional concepts of dramatic simulation and play can be transformed by technology and media into the arena of digital games, particularly those based on role-play and virtual worlds.

## Drama, technology and education

Some drama educators may note the subtitle of this book with some trepidation but they need not anticipate another apology for the technological determinism so often used as a reason for unthinking change. The traditional values of drama are to be valued even more in a time of often unlooked-for technological transformation. This ambivalence towards technology is expressed in popular terms through a series of oppositional positions within western culture. Despite the current unpopularity of dualities in some theoretical circles, the arts and technology debate often makes people fall into oppositional camps.

As Michael Foucault (1986) says: '...everything is dangerous, nothing is innocent'; all things reflect some value judgment or ideology. Some people still set technology and drama in opposition, which is evidence of the ideological tension in the educational system and reflects the cultural anxiety about technological change.

The tension can be expressed as: drama *versus* technology, art *versus* industry, sensitivity *versus* brutalism, high culture *versus* low culture.

These dualities are partly a reflection of the modernist view which positions educated people as sensitively attuned to high culture, including drama, and uneducated people as mindlessly enslaved to low culture entertainment. This view is still part of the popular discourse on technology, for example the multi-billion dollar global video games industry:

> Video games today find themselves in the position that cinema and jazz occupied before the Second World War: popular but despised, thought to be beneath serious evaluation. (Poole, 2000, p26)

These cultural dualities are no longer relevant given the pervasiveness of technology in the lives of young people. Currently, students inhabit a global culture with a range of digital technologies and media forms at their disposal. They negotiate their own learning and leisure, using a range of screen-based digital hardware that displays performances and texts which they can constantly interact with so that their sense of place in society is mediated through and produced by their interaction with this technology. This is not a one-way interaction: they take those aspects they want and reshape them for their own pleasures and ends.

## Beyond hype

There has been an unfortunate tendency by educators and educational administrators to be short-sighted about the claims made by the computer industry about technology (Cuban, 2001). Predictably, every new product will provide solutions to an educator's problem. This chapter provides a more critical view of technology and its application to drama education. We believe that ideally education should be making demands of and shaping technology, not the other way around. We believe, like Jaron Lanier (quoted in Powell, 1996), in a

...balanced attitude towards technology and aesthetics, in which you neither shy away from nor worship technology, but enjoy the rush of being able to create entirely new things with it...

This vitality is evident in the case studies used throughout the book.

This chapter begins the discussion about the potential of shared space for drama and technology. In other chapters we tie the theoretical discussion about technology and drama to case studies of actual projects undertaken by the authors and others. Quite apart from the debate about whether technology is good for education or not, there is no longer a choice. Young people will automatically engage with technologies they grow up with in the home such as their telephones, their computers and their televisions. Everyday technology is not questioned by students in the drama classroom, as it is an integral part of their lives.

How can we harness this cultural acceptance of and comfort with technology to meet the needs of our drama students and use it to make exciting and useful virtual worlds combining drama and technology?

Drama education has insights to offer media content developers in understanding how to create viable, interesting and meaningful virtual worlds. John Carroll noted with irony that two conferences held in Bergen, Norway in 2002 took place at the same time: one of drama educators and one of digital arts theorists and practitioners. If only the two had intermingled. The creation of virtual reality is something drama educators have been developing research and theory on since the early 1960s. The world of computer gaming seems oblivious of the developments in process drama. Marie-Laure Ryan in her book *Narrative as Virtual Reality* (2001, p305) says:

> When performing becomes synonymous with living, the theatrical experience inherits the immersive and interactive qualities that define our experience of being-in-the-world. This fusion of life and representation and this total engagement of the actors are of course far too utopian to offer any kind of useful guidelines for the developers of interactive art.

The essence of drama education is the ability to hold two worlds in the mind at the same time and thus understand real life through the dramatic and virtual (Boal, 1995, p42-43). While this may be utopian to Ryan, it is the daily work of drama educators. The language and structures sought by constructors of virtual realities already exist and could be used to understand the development of authentic and engaging new worlds. The growing interest of educators in the serious application of digital games technology as a learning tool should lead to the existing knowledge surrounding drama in education, especially process drama.

## Creating mediated learning communities

As figure 1.1 illustrates, our premise in this book is that technology and media can act as a transforming agent for traditional forms in the broad field of drama and learning. We believe this can produce a new hybrid, mediated learning environment. This is not to say that the existing models of practice are not valid and worthwhile. In many cases they are the only option for experiencing drama in a learning environment that lacks or chooses not to use technology.

## Drama and learning

By drama and learning we mean to encompass the range of activities that are usually covered by the spectrum of educational practices that have been more traditionally known as drama in education, theatre studies and theatre in education. This area has been chosen because within popular culture the omnibus concept of drama in all its manifestations has been radically affected by the continuing technological and media changes that are transforming the cultural landscape. It is useful to examine how these changes could affect the educationally based forms of drama in this time of rapid change.

## Process drama, performance and games

Within the wide range of educational practices that constitute drama and theatrical form we focus on three forms. First, process drama, drama in education or creative dramatics, as it is variously known, has been chosen because it is closely aligned to curriculum outcomes and educational practice in a wide range of learning environments. It has had a strong theoretical and practical development over the last sixty years and has developed a range of techniques that are particularly well developed to make use of technological change. As more educators and instructional designers begin to consider emerging learning technology systems such as the development of 'serious' video games, they might benefit by considering the existing knowledge and practices in this area of drama. We believe that there are definite links between the principles, practices and conventions of process drama developed over several decades, and the learning systems being considered in the emerging areas of what is variously being referred to serious games, 'epistemic' games (Shaffer *et al*, 2005) or 'curricular' games (Prensky, 2006).

Secondly, in this context, performance means the process and development of dramatic work for an audience. Our focus here is on work created for and

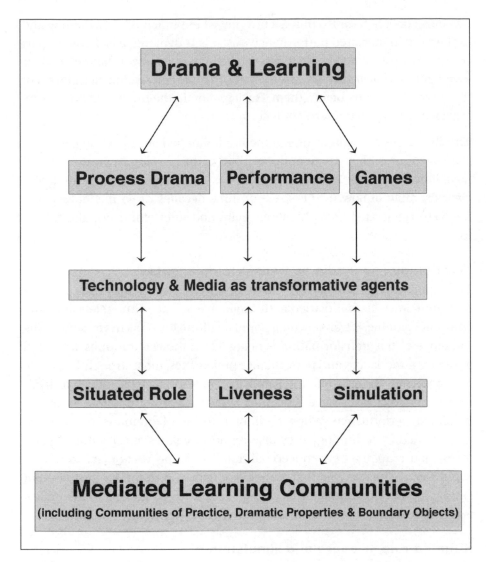

**Figure 1.1**

by young people because that is currently where much of the vibrancy and excitement in mediated performance exists. This dynamism is driven in part by the desire of young people to see and be in performances that reflect their own cultural *milieu* and not just the performance conventions and forms of those who have gone before them. Participation in the process of art making is seen as central to modern audiences.

Thirdly, games are seen as one of the fundamental learning strategies of all human cultures. They are an important part of the learning environment, and have long been incorporated into drama as a learning tool. They are also a clear example of how in the space of three decades or so technology and media has generated a new, highly engaging and entertaining popular culture form.

## Technology and media as transforming agents

The exponential growth of technology, especially in the digital forms of entertainment and dramatic media through live event, film, television and computer gaming, is transforming popular culture forms as never before. The influence of this transformation is being felt in the classroom as well as in audience attendances and performance preferences, most strongly by people of school age. For example mediated 'live' performances at music festivals means audience sizes have grown far beyond anything possible at an unmediated performance. When traditional forms of dramatic practice are transformed by technology they take on new qualities and produce hybrid forms that require a new conceptual framework and vocabulary to understand them. The changes that technology makes to dramatic form are not simply an add-on; a qualitative change occurs which generates theoretical issues based on role and performance that need exploring.

## Situated role, liveness and simulation

*Situated Role* is the term used in this book to describe how process drama operates when it is combined with the computer-mediated technologies of the Internet and other technologies. By using a digital pretext (Carroll, 2004), the drama combines with digital content and allows the students to develop virtual expertise while operating online. This form of drama has much in common with serious games and Dorothy Heathcote's Commission Model detailed in chapter 3. The drama takes on some of the qualities of situated understanding and learning (Lave and Wenger, 1991) because it is able to access the expertise of communities of practice that exist in the online world.

## Liveness

*Liveness* is a term used by Philip Auslander (1999) to describe the technologically heightened awareness of live human presence in performance. Auslander suggests that before humankind had the ability to record video and audio, the concept of liveness did not exist. He argues that there is an inexorable shift toward live and mediated performance converging:

> But what interests me are more subtle transformations in the live event itself, which makes it more like a media event ... the audience's expectations of what they'll see live are formed by their experience of television and film, not by a history of seeing live performances ... Live theatre will always be live, I think, but it will also start to look more and more like other, more popular, mediatized forms. (Harju, 1997)[4]

The implication for drama educators is that performance developed by and for students is now more than ever likely to be influenced, created and performed in conjunction with media. According to Auslander almost all performance is now influenced in its style and content by mediatisation. From the humble microphone in an intimate 'live' venue to the bombardment of video images at a rock concert, the live event is now mediated.

The mediation of live games and play raises issues concerning simulation. In our interpretation, simulations do not have to be predictive models about the real world. Rather, we are talking about the extent to which mediated games such as computer and video games can represent a particular mediated experience. For example, playing chess against a physically present player presents a fundamentally different experience to that of playing a computer software-based adversary in an online game of chess. While the rules, goals and strategies remain the same, the experience is altered by the interface used to play the game.

At the highest levels of simulation, technology and media are used to create high-fidelity models with the aim of representing a real world experience as accurately as possible. But low fidelity representations can be just as engaging if the nature of the thing being simulated is captured, as evidenced by the popularity of the early video game *Pong* as a representation of a tennis match using just two on-screen lines as paddles, and a dot for a ball.

A whole range of activities are open to simulation using technology and media but the resulting experiences for the players will be inherently different. The challenge for those wishing to use technology and games within mediated learning communities is to capture the essence of the real world event, task or activity to be simulated. Then, even relatively low-level classroom-based simulations can be highly effective and engaging.

## Mediated learning communities

Mediated learning communities are the dramatic structures that are developed when the forms of process drama, performance and games are transformed by technology. While retaining much of their original form, they have a range of new and interesting qualities that can be used in the broader drama and learning context. The ability of technology, via computer mediated communication, to provide access not only to information but also to a vast range of online communities allows for the development of mediated learning communities. These mediated learning communities are communities based on common interest and expertise rather than spatial locatedness. They use the everyday technology of computer-based communication to establish centres of expertise that can be used as real world digital pretexts for dramatically situated learning.

## Communities of practice

Within process drama scenarios situated in communities of practice (Wenger, 1998), the online mediated learning community approach allows young people who are involved to interact with the authentic learning vocabulary and information of such communities. As virtual apprentices they can master the required content of the subject material under examination and develop a situated understanding of the context. Learners can understand complex concepts inherent in the material while remaining protected by the situated dramatic role they have assumed within the drama. By accessing real communities of practice while dramatically framed through role distance, they are able to enter what Shaffer (2004) calls the 'epistemic frame' of the community of practice. This enables them to access the body of knowledge and ways of thinking and acting that individuals learn and contribute to when they become part of a specific community of practice.

## Dramatic property

A *dramatic property* (Paul Sutton, C&T, personal communication, 2005) represents a transcodification (Tulloch, 2000) of content from one dramatic form to another. This concept, which is the core intellectual property developed from a dramatic performance, is seen as transferable to all forms of digital representation including technology, such as theatre and music events, digital games, computers and mobile phones as well as with dramatic and linguistic modes such as texting and chat rooms. By integrating the dramatic property across a range of technological platforms, it taps into a new aesthetic based on the multimodal use of intellectual content operating through the audience's technoliteracy skills.

The 'dramatic property' is already part of mainstream media thinking but has not yet been applied in a systematic way to work developing from a drama and learning base. Within the theatre and entertainment industry, a level of vertical integration operates, which means that a 'dramatic property' can transfer from an animated film to a live stage show to a video game or an illustrated comic. The transcodification of Disney's *The Lion King* from animated film to live performance is a good example of how a dramatic property can operate across different media. The intellectual product is at the core of the dramatic property, which can transfer across different modes of dramatising media generating energy, cross promotion and audiences.

## Boundary objects

The term *boundary object* (Star, 1989) describes objects that co-ordinate different perspectives towards a particular purpose. It is used in discussion of communities of practice (Wenger, 1998) as a way of understanding how communities can function or cooperate with external organisations. Boundary objects provide a common artifact that serves different purposes or provides different meanings to individuals within a community, or between communities.

As one possible product of transcodifying games through technology into a simulation, computer and video games are boundary objects. For example, a video game like *The Sims* could be considered the technological transformation of some elements of doll play or puppetry. As a boundary object, *The Sims* represents different things to members of a learning community: a teacher may see it as a way of learning about relationships, while a student may see it as the platform for recording and creating scenes to be edited later into a short film parodying television sitcoms.

This has all been made possible by a new generation of young people who have swum in an ever-deepening pool of technology since their earliest days. Marc Prensky (2001b) calls this generation in drama education classrooms now: 'digital natives'.

## Digital Natives

As former Disney executive Alan Kay observes, '...technology is only technology if it was invented after you were born' (Prensky, 2001a, p38). This comment is typical of the axiom that new technology is the domain of the *next* generation, a presumption that sees otherwise authoritative adults willing to venerate teenagers as the only people capable of fully understanding new devices. The often-used example from the pre-DVD age was of parents having to humbly call upon their teenage children to change the clock setting on the video cassette recorder.

Attempts to place current students into a generational taxonomy have tended to focus on their relationship with technology. Students born in the early 1980s are the *net generation* (Tapscott, 1998; Oblinger and Oblinger, 2005), or even the *nintendo generation* (Green, Reid and Bigum, 1998). The *millennial generation* (Strauss and Howe, 1997) are characterised by their fascination with technology, their ability to multitask, their expectations of fast inter-action with information and their desire for connectivity – both physically and virtually (Oblinger and Oblinger, 2005).

Prensky's *Digital Game Based Learning* (2001a) trumpets the most evan-gelical of claims that educators must now deal with the 'games generation'. He contends that people under the age of 30 have grown up with digital tech-nology and are proficient with its applications. Dealing primarily with cor-porate training, Prensky assumes that on average most trainers are older than trainees and that often there is a generational/technological chasm between teachers and learners. For example, the current teaching generation grew up with books, linear film and television, vinyl records and wired telephones. The games generation has grown up with video games, MTV music clips, CDs, the Internet, and mobile phones. Students are digital natives whereas their teachers are digital immigrants (Prensky, 2001b).

Young people are not interested in technology for technology's sake but seek out technologies that will enhance their lifestyles. Recent research by Carroll and Peck *et al*, (2002, p58) suggests that young people appropriate technology to '...add value to their lifestyles, satisfy their social and leisure needs and reinforce their group identity'. Additionally they found that technology was heavily influenced by the situation of use. These findings raise some signi-ficant challenges for those examining the place of technology in education. How can MP3 players, digital video cameras and computer games be used to greater effect in the drama classroom?

Drama can and does exist in a bare studio without media or technological enhancement, although this is increasingly rare in the commercial world of theatre. However, an important premise of this book is that technology and drama produce hybrid new forms to augment what can be achieved by imagination alone.

## The Commission Model and situated role:
## an example of transformation

Let's consider the transformative effect of technology on process drama as an example of the new mediated learning communities that can be created by this change.

Process drama sees the process of performance as the learning objective rather than the actual product. It uses role-based performance to engage learners at an emotional level, often bringing them into communities of practice based on research and imagination. Developed since the mid 20th century, a recent application of its principles can be seen in 'A Vision Possible: The Commission Model of Teaching' (Heathcote, 2003). Her article is a case study of one such dramatically framed community of practice developed by Dorothy Heathcote as an alternative model of educational organisation.

Heathcote describes how a community of students was commissioned with the responsibility of designing the garden of a newly completed hospital. This was a real commission as the garden was to be used by patients, staff and visitors when the hospital was opened. Setting up the dramatic frame allowed the students to assume the role status of garden designers. This provided natural routes into talking, reading, writing and particularly into developing confidence in a public voice related to the design and delivery of the garden. Students were able, when dramatically framed, to enter the world of professional practice of architect and landscape gardener and adopt the epistemic frame of such specialists within the virtual world developed through the drama. As Heathcote says about such drama;

> ...it is above all a social art, and places the human 'face' and affairs of humans at its very centre... A strong emphasis upon dramatic experiences of many kinds brings these additional elements to the fore, a strong emphasis upon tasks, in social circumstances, with a sense of productive tension regarding forms, disciplines, selectivity of behaviour and language. The main drama elements are the development of the self-spectator, the shaping of the work in action and the emergence of reflective monitoring during the work. (Heathcote, 2003, p17)

The principles of the Commission Model could be summarised as:

■ Throughout the work the participants carry the 'client' in their head
This is the future audience for communication, demonstration and answering questions. There is an absence of institutionalised pupil talk or teacher talk

Language has to be found in practice, it is a collaboration between the commissioner's skills and knowledge

■ There is no pre-planned curriculum map

Research into the problem dictates a varied and complex curriculum based on the needs of the commission

■ Time scales matter

Projects need to carry the work forward over long time spans even if drama time is in short bursts

■ Tasks are formulated by the needs of the commission

This requires flexibility as tasks are designed to fit need and the terms and time available

■ Ordering of study is driven by commission requirements

Information in depth is concentrated on the tasks to be completed

■ All completed task work 'banked' to be reused and developed

Classification and access to information are important for new insights

■ The learning environment is dynamic

Digital tools, phones, computers and the Internet as well as constantly reconfiguring the physical environment are used to meet task requirements.

■ Openness to participant's contributions is valued

Language used is based on task contribution not power or status.

(Adapted from Heathcote, 2003, p18)

The Commission Model provides a sense of authenticity and responsibility precisely because although it is dramatically framed, there are real clients with real requirements and the final work is published and acted on. The actual implementation of the project may be passed on to specialists to complete. With young pupils, their parents and teachers can act as internal publishers and the work is then presented to the wider school community.

Essentially the Commission Model is about engaging students with a community of practice (Wenger, 1998). These communities, existing in the wider world of work, are where much real learning in our society occurs. A community of practice is a specific group with a local culture, what James Gee describes as a way of '...seeing, valuing, and being in the world' (2005, para 5). These communities of practice provide participants with a common repertoire of knowledge about and ways of addressing shared problems and purposes (Lave and Wenger, 1991). One of the interesting shifts has been that in the past communities of practice were bound by spatial boundaries and proximity. With the advent of the online world, communities of practice sprang up that were based on shared interest, not shared location. They have now developed in such a way that a relatively obscure interest or hobby will most likely have an online community of practice.

Not everyone has the *cachet*, contacts, times or resources to develop real commissions using the Commission Model of process drama, particularly beyond school boundaries. If access to more complex communities of practice than school resources can provide is required, real expertise or specialised knowledge is readily and freely available on the Web. Wikipedia is a good example. When students involved in one of the case studies outlined in Chapter 6 were searching for answers to questions relating to marine archaeology they found them in a community of practice accessed through the Wikipedia: Community Portal at (http://en.wikipedia.org/wiki/Wiki pedia: Community_Portal#Active_collaborations). For more information about how collaborative software such as a wiki works, see the Wikipedia entry at http://en.wikipedia.org/wiki/Wiki. The material was available at the interactive and individual level via blogs and specialist sites. Using the resources of the online world, time can be collapsed and projects made flexible if students have access to computers. After all, students are only at school for five hours a day and many of them already spend hours a day playing online games. The Web provides free digital publishing, including images, audio and video and setting up a site is now relatively simple. An example of a digital pretext and online induction into junior commission role using everyday technologies of e-mail, Weblogs and forum postings is examined in detail in Chapter 6's review of the *To the Spice Islands* project.

Through using readily available technology the aims of the Commission Model can be maintained while the high level of resource and time pressure on teachers and institutions is eased. Busy teachers will have time to plan, and classroom project sessions can move quickly because a lot of the thinking and initial work for the project can be done outside the classroom.

The use of these online communities of practice helps to answer another problem of how to arrange access to those professionals who constitute the body of knowledge of professional practice in an area of expertise. If you were interested in studying urban design with your students, where would you access resources and how would the professional designer find the time to teach your students? Using mediated learning communities to locate Websites and groups interested in urban design, teaching can still work within these real world restrictions.

The cross platform digital technologies of computers, gaming simulations, hand held communication devices and the Internet allow students to access the expertise of professional communities of practice in a way never before possible. This digital world does not work on 40-minute blocks; it is running on continuous global time, and is constantly updated. It is the world of real communities of practice. Access to expertise is available online to pupils at their level of interest, from the most basic information to the most complex. Information is available online on 'how engines work' for pre-schoolers and nuclear physicists and for almost everyone in between. Whatever the student's entry level into a community of practice, there is the potential for professional, non-patronising, real world information offering solutions to genuine tasks. The newly developed digital technologies make it possible to develop a new range of dramatically framed progressive pedagogies of practice that make use of situated role.

## Video games for authentic learning: the links between process drama and 'serious' games

This chapter concludes with a brief introduction of how educators interested in the application of technology to learning may be converging towards similar forms of work which are already well understood by their drama education colleagues.

Shaffer and Resnick (1999) describe 'thickly authentic' learning contexts, in which the learner uses real tools, knowledge and practices to address issues they care about. A more difficult prospect is the creation of an environment in which this type of learning can occur, where the interests and concerns of the learners are aligned with a domain of knowledge, authentic and valued practices and modes of assessment. As Shaffer says, 'In thickly authentic settings content is freely accessible, and motivation is easy. Creating thickly authentic environments though is hard' (Shaffer, 2005, p1).

However, there is a large body of expertise and experience in the educational drama world which has worked to create thickly authentic settings with few resources and limited budgets and has developed a wide range of techniques for doing it. Drama teachers also know that developing thickly authentic learning environments in schools has always been difficult because these ways of working are largely absent from school curriculum. Much of the traditional school curriculum still operates on the basis of a transmission model of educational practice. These models, as Shaffer says, are derived from '...medieval scholarship constituted within schools developed in the industrial revolution' (Shaffer and Gee, 2005, p24). Part of the problem is that the industrial time management model of classroom practice discourages a range of innovative teaching including drama teaching. Children need to have time to think and work in depth in a community of practice if they are to grapple with complex problems. This cannot be accomplished in 40 minute chunks of time, which are then assessed by standardised tests.

Teachers have long known that the most authentic contexts for learning involve becoming a participant in a community of practice; yet practical constraints such as access and time have limited the extent to which this can occur in traditional schooling. The apprenticeship model is generally applied post-school/pre-career. One way to simulate this immersion is to use the power of the new technologies to enter the skills and knowledge of a community. These are '...the conventions of participation that individuals internalise when they become acculturated' (Shaffer, 2005, p1) to a community's way of thinking. Engaging with real knowledge, for example via the resources of the Internet, can enhance the authenticity of role-based dramatic play. Students who are dramatically framed within virtual communities can work and think in innovative ways as professionals within a virtual community.

Shaffer, Gee and others discuss a form of learning based on what they call 'epistemic' games. They see the potential to apply technology and appropriate learning systems from some digital games to create a learning environment that places students within a virtual professional community of practice. Shaffer (2005) describes a scenario in which students learn about town planning by using professional software, acting in role as city planners, and producing plans which they present to a representative from the city planning office. To drama educators familiar with process drama, the parallels are obvious. The *Madison 2200* project described by Shaffer is a model of how Dorothy Heathcote's Commission Model might work with the application of technology.

The similarities between epistemic games and the Commission Model lie in the application of a process to a task that has been derived from a community of practice; for example garden design will need access to the world of garden designers. The Commission Model uses process drama and situated role, while the epistemic games approach uses digital games to make these connections. The epistemic games model is directly connected to the technologically driven computer games movement whilst the Commission Model draws on the powerful traditions of drama and theatre. The epistemic games movement calls for 'richly authentic settings', while the Commission Model actually provides those settings for students to work within. This convergence of thinking from very different educational perspectives demonstrates the synergies between drama and games, situated role and simulation, process drama and epistemic games.

## Conclusion

Drama teachers who understand the emerging performance conventions inherent in mediated learning communities can use them to engage their students to explore authenticity and role-based identity in new ways. At the same time teachers can make use of the connection between the shifting conventions of live theatre and the digital performance modes evolving around it. They will then be able to connect with their students and contemporary artistic representations of identity in a digital world of increasing image and text overload. Because they are uniquely positioned as specialists in performance within the school curriculum, drama teachers are able to look at this evolving digital world with a critical eye, not to dismiss it, because it will not go away. Neither do drama teachers have to embrace the rush to the virtual pushed by technological determinists. They are acutely aware that the physical body is now the central place of conflict in our society. Tattoos and the body piercing which are popular with young people are signs of the struggle for ownership and control being fought out in both real and virtual worlds.

The importance of the work of the drama teacher in a school environment and curriculum structure which has not yet caught up with the technological changes of the present day cannot be overestimated. In an increasingly fragmented and media-based world, new audiences will continue to want the truth of theatre and the authenticity of drama. It remains the task of the drama teacher/artists to adapt the conditions evolving in both the digital world and the area of live theatre to their classrooms and find strategies that work.

In Chapter 2 we examine the dominant popular culture forms young people are engaging with and discuss how drama educators can move beyond the basic use of technology to create meaningful learning experiences in drama education. Drama educators are well placed to support their students in their evolving role as both makers and appreciators of culture in contemporary society.

## Notes

1 This quote taken from an interview on ABC Radio National in 2004. The whole talk can be accessed at http://www.abc.net.au/rn/talks/bbing/

2 For a full account of the Batavia shipwreck and its aftermath, Mike Dash's *Batavia's Graveyard* (2002) provides a definitive and highly readable narrative.

3 This transcript is translated from http://anmrc.blogpsot.com, a blog created for the Spice Island's project detailed in Chapter 5.

4 This interview can be found at http://www.teak.fi/teak/ACT/auslander.html

# 2
## Changing forms of drama

D igital media works by sampling information. The average music CD features more than 44,000 samples of sound every second, providing a reasonably detailed representation of the music, or at least of changes in volume and the frequencies within the range of average human ears. But a series of digital samples can never be a fully accurate representation of continuous real-world data, just as this book could never claim to be a complete representation of all the subtle ways in which technology, drama and education constantly intersect and refine each other over time.

Technology is a rapidly moving target. In offering examples of how particular technology can be applied to performance there is a real risk of being quickly sidelined by the rapid take-up of what the computer industry quaintly terms the next *killer application*. Much valuable recent research into digital role performance and identity is based on early online environments such as Multi-User Dungeons (MUDs) and Multi-Object Orientations (MOOs). These text-based virtual worlds now seem positively steam-driven compared to the latest 3D graphics-powered video games, virtual worlds and computer-generated visual effects seen in film and television.

Drama appears to move at a much slower pace. Its basic forms are familiar to us from Aeschylus to Andrew Lloyd-Webber, from *Hamlet* to *The Lion King*. But dramatic forms are not as static as they might appear, especially in a world flush with mobile, screen-based, networked, interactive media. There are many challenges for drama teachers who must deal with a generation of students whose perceptions and expectations of drama may be quite different from their own.

This chapter offers samples of the interplay between technology and drama and examines how these cultural elements might bridge, rather than widen, the gap between teachers and their students. John Carroll recalls such a moment from the nineties:

> I took a break between sessions at a National Drama Conference in Canberra, Australia some years ago to visit the nearby cinema multiplex where *Terminator II: Judgment Day* was playing. It stars Arnold Schwarzenegger and a range of digital special effects. Arnold plays a cyborg with no moral sensibility and no pain threshold; however he does possess a very appealing sense of mission. His job involved him in protecting a young boy he has been sent back from the future to save.

> If this time paradox does not make sense I suggest you hire the DVD, get in some popcorn and watch it for yourself! However, you really had to be there with the big screen, the Dolby Surround sound and the audience participation to get the full impact.

> It was clear from their response that the young audience I saw the film with had no trouble with the space/time paradox, and at the moment of cyborg-Arnold's supreme sacrifice a sense of catharsis was plainly and appreciatively evident in the theatre.

> I returned to the conference ready to discuss my enthusiasm for drama, computers and cyberspace. I ended up engaged in an animated, if somewhat sceptical, discussion about drama and technology with the conference delegates.

> However, I felt I was on to something about role and identity, and sensed that the growing relationship between the dramatic digital world and real life performance was part of a larger cultural change now in progress.

## Drama in an age of digital reproduction

Teachers/artists working in the field of educational drama are surrounded by a world increasingly dominated by screen-mediated images. Many teachers are concerned about how, as drama educators, they can connect with their students and the current forms of mediated artistic representation that are so popular with them. This seems increasingly difficult in a digital world of image and text overload. This chapter discusses questions of performance and aesthetics and the changing audience perceptions of drama among young people.

These concerns parallel another time when this influence of technology on artistic production was a central issue: the sub-heading of this section is an ironic reference to Walter Benjamin's famous 1936 paper, *The work of art in the age of mechanical reproduction* (Benjamin, 1969). In this highly influential article Benjamin discusses the changes that had occurred in audience reception in the arts in his day. He considers how photography and especially film had changed the form of theatre, drama and the fine arts.

Benjamin felt that the authenticity of the individual artwork, whether it was fine art or drama, would be degraded by the ease of constant reproduction by mechanical means such as photography and film. Benjamin nevertheless finds the effects of media mass culture liberating and looks forward to the breakdown of the rituals of artistic practice. This has, of course, not happened. Recognised original artworks or international theatre productions have become increasingly valuable as their rarity and celebrity status produces a monetary value that places them outside any connection to national cultural or economic systems. Reproduction did not equal degradation as Benjamin had thought, instead his worst fears about celebrity were being realised. As Marxist modernism waned, something else was going on culturally. This was the rise of a new audience, both for the reproductions of images of art as still photography and as filmed drama, as well as for celebrity artist/performers who by performing in them transcended their national backgrounds and became international stars. Mechanical reproduction of images enabled global celebrity on a scale previously unimagined.

However the danger, which Benjamin identified, and as John E. McGrath (2004, p167) points out, was,

> ...that modern subjects, rather than finding themselves in a self aware spatial relation to contemporary culture, would instead be manipulated into overwhelmed, self-annihilating fascination with the unapproachable excess of the mass-produced cultural artifact.

Seventy years on, and despite such fears, digital reproduction has become a dominant form of production across all fields of artistic endeavor, including the filmic and dramatic. The mediatised image has replaced the live performance as the generator of income within the cultural economy just as live performance has incorporated the virtual into its repertoire of effects (Auslander, 1999, p39). This transformation has produced another generational shift in audiences that are now accessing digital content through the computer, the DVD and interactive hand-held devices including mobile telephones. This dominance of mediatised reproductions of performance has led live performance to employ digital technologies that mimic the collapse of distance and the close-up intimacy of the mediatised image and sound produced by DVD. Even such traditional performance forms as Gilbert and

Sullivan operettas often use radio-microphone enhanced performers, allowing the audience to catch every nuance of the song, even when it is performed in a music hall venue that does not require such enhancement.

The questions posed by drama teachers about changing audience perceptions of drama seem similar and even more urgent today than they were for Walter Benjamin, partly because the pace of technological change and information obsolescence is so much faster now. Teacher/artists are working today in schools with young people who inhabit a world saturated with mediated digital images and interactive technologies that are entertainment, identity maintenance and communication devices all at the same time.

## A Marxist Theatre in Education

Benjamin's solution to the new audience perception of multiple image reproduction was radical for its time. He imagined an improvised drama pedagogy that would affect the total life of the child, challenge the boundaries of middle-class separation and isolation of conventional education as well as counter the predominance of mass-produced image (Zipes, 1973, p22-24). The ability of dramatic convention to transform objects and expose the reification of experience through the 'radical release of play' (Benjamin, 1973, p31) was seen as a way forward by Benjamin and others. Young people's theatre was seen as a way to overcome the growing commodification of artistic cultural product, especially the commercial theatre that was seen to naturalise the capitalistic form delivered by mass culture (Kershaw, 1999, p23).

Rather idealistically, Benjamin hoped that this theatre-in-education process would expose the separation of public and private domains and allow new social freedoms to exist for young people along with the new technology. The failure to take into account the growth of the global arts economy meant this dream was doomed to failure. The pressures of technology, globalisation and the accompanying commodification of artistic form that are a part of technological change continued to dominate theatre and led ultimately to the internationalisation of performance. This can be seen most clearly in musical theatre where musicals such as Cameron Mackintosh's *Miss Saigon* or Disney's *The Lion King* occupy top billing in cities around the world. Paradoxically, this trend has encouraged a cross-cultural conformism and has been accelerated by international media advertising to produce a global market for this kind of theatre. The ritual of spectacle consumer theatre attendance has never been greater.

In Baz Kershaw's analysis, by embracing the disciplines of the new consumerism, the popular established theatre has succumbed '...to a commodification that stifles radicalism in the moment of its birth' (Kershaw, 1999, p23) or at a subsidised national level has become a formulaic comedy of manners for an *elite* aging clientele. But there is certainly still an *avant-garde* fringe and a range of high-level international performers that produce high-art festival and celebrity performances for a rich global audience in an increasingly commodified market place.

## A new aesthetic

Today this commodified theatre is a major form of entertainment around the world. However, as Paul Virilio points out, in the digital world of computers, gaming, video and mobile telephones, we are all, and especially young people, '...directors of our own reality' (Virilio, 1989, p66) and there are many other alternative forms of mediatised performance available. This collapse of the distance between participant and spectator, encouraged in forms of mediated drama, shifts the viewing aesthetic and the audience from being passive to active and towards some dynamic interaction with the content of the performance. The mediated drama of television, especially reality and event television and computer gaming are affective: we interact with them, influence their outcomes and are emotionally connected to their outcomes via the developing interface culture (Johnson, 1997, p24) typified by mobile telephones.

In contrast to the mediated forms of entertainment and communication such as television and video gaming, which are available for young people, there is still a wide range of theatre, with various levels of 'liveness' (Auslander, 1999) available with its inbuilt discipline of the theatre space and the closed performance text (de Marinis, 1987, p52) encouraging audience spectatorship. Despite this wide variety, mainstream theatre seems increasingly remote from the concerns of a young audience engaged in a complex round of interactive mediated drama on a variety of screens and digital platforms typified by such television shows such as *Big Brother*. This young audience expects to have some say in the results of these performances as they identify with the concerns about identity and authenticity they raise. These concerns take on a new urgency when combined with the fluidity and 'openness' of digital performance conventions (Cameron and Carroll, 2004, p68).

It is difficult for drama teachers to provide the connection to the exciting physical art form of theatre and make it seem relevant in a world where digital editing is seen by many as the preferred form of artistic expression. From rip, mix and burn to scratch, dub and hip-hop, the digital image and sound mix performances, either homage or plagiarism, depending on your position, are the artistic forms of choice for the new young audience.

## Cultural media environment

Nevertheless, the question remains as to why such performances, including event, reality and surveillance drama are so popular with young audiences. This popularity seems to be related to the fact that for the current generation of young people, the digital mediation of the Internet, convergent telephony and digital video are not seen as separate technologies but as part of their cultural environment As already noted, technology is only seen as technology if it was invented after you were born. As science fiction and comedy writer Douglas Adams (2001) said:

> Anything that's invented after you're 35 is against the natural order of things ... Anything that's in the world when you were born is considered ordinary and normal.

The most obvious and intrusive form that has evolved is the mobile telephone and its subsequent cultural appropriation by young people. The preferred form of usage is the short message service (SMS), which has evolved a language and subculture of its own. In Australia 3.9 billion text messages were sent in 2003. A lot of them were interactive voting for 'event reality' TV shows such as *Big Brother* or the *Pop Idol* series. This convergent technology connects communication and role-based performance in a new way as well as connecting young people to each other in a growing communication network.

This platform, with its associated new digital forms of wireless broadband radio and photo imaging, has continued to evolve and merge with video gaming and Internet access. Combining this with the 16.7 hours a week spent on the Web, 13.6 for television and 12 hours a week for radio, the evolving media ecology of young people starts to look different from those in Benjamin's world. In the 2003 Yahoo and Carat Interactive study reported in Bainbridge (2004), 50 per cent of respondents said they consume multiple media at once, watching television or listening to the radio while surfing the Internet. Interestingly enough the television watched was largely drama-based soaps or reality based programmes. These young people are the digital natives that Marc Prensky (2001b) speaks of.

## Connecting young people to drama

In connecting young people, drama specialists in schools always start with the cultural environment of the student and through drama hope to introduce them to a more critical and reflective take on role and performance. Maybe the first element in reestablishing the connection between live theatre audiences and a young digital audience is to become aware of how the cultural ecologies of live and mediated performance influence each other as digital reproduction continues to expand. If we can understand this relationship, teachers and artists may be able to engage with the current aesthetic and design work that will go some way to answering the question of student focus and engagement within the dramatic arts.

The interdependence of artistic response to the newly evolving digital culture of theatrical practice has not so far been widely discussed. The main focus has usually been the adoption of improvised role to so-called *reality and event performance* (Carroll, 2002). However the digital/multimedia influence is evident when other currently popular forms of the theatre are considered. The preferences of the digital generation audience have begun to influence live performance as clearly as the mechanical and cinematic reproduction of images did in the theatres of the 1930s and 1940s. Bertolt Brecht is a clear example of the influence of media forms within performance during this time, as was his rejection of realism as a contemporary dramatic form. Unlike Benjamin's idealistic socialist dream for student drama in this same period, Brecht's emphasis on media and stylised performance resonated with the technologically literate western audience, even if his politics didn't.

Today this same relationship between *avant-garde* live performance and digital performance, especially interactive role forms, can be summed up by the preferences of the current young audiences as seen in the following diagram.

**Table 2.1 Digital Generation Audiences**

|  | Live Performance Audience | Digital Performance Audience |
|---|---|---|
| Preferred cultural form | Collaborative and physical | Mediated and virtual |
| Entertainment expectation | Interpretative and non-naturalistic | Configurative and interactive |
| Underlying assumptions | Acceptance of ambiguity in text | Acceptance of open narrative |
| Production preference | Spectacle and intertextual layering | Interaction and appropriation as art form |

These shifts in audience expectations were first seen in experimental work in fringe theatre and have increasingly moved to the mainstream. As happened with Brecht, the mainstream theatre will always catch up with the *avant-garde* and incorporate it into the dominant theatrical forms of the culture (Featherstone, 1991, p36). The emerging cultural forms of live performance have shifted towards the collaborative and physical in response to the growth of a performance emphasis on disembodied, constructed and mutable identity. The success of drama groups such as *Cirque du Soleil* or Circus Oz and individual artists such as Ariane Mnouchkine or Robert Lepage also point to this trend in international celebrity live theatre.

Within digital performance the avatar role-based forms of Massively Multi-player Online Role Playing Games such as *EverQuest* and *Diablo* emphasise the interactive and transformative nature of the role performance. The intensity of the physical performance in much current theatre, exemplified by groups such as *La Fura dels Baus* sets up and counterpoints an alternative reality to that of the intensity of the vicariously experienced, screen-based roles now available online.

### Preferences of young audiences

The entertainment expectation of the younger live audience is for inter-pretative and non-naturalistic forms both in performance roles and pro-duction design. This is matched by an expectation in digital performance that any involvement will be configurative and interactive. That is, the spectator/participant will have to work or interact with the performance for it to happen at all. In learning terms, Eskelinen (2001) makes a critical distinction between this sort of activity-based learning and that of engaging in traditional text-based learning. He makes the point that the dominant mode of learning in literature, mainstream theatre, and film is interpretative, while in games and process drama it is configurative. He says '...in art we might have to configure in order to able to interpret whereas in games we have to interpret in order to configure' (Eskelinen, 2001, p2).

By this he means that in the process of playing a game such as *EverQuest*, players are engaged in the construction of an individual and unique screen-based semiotic structure and their role within it. This consists of a selective configuration of the game elements and their own player choices. The wide-ranging variable expression of meaning built into a non-linear game text that need to be interpreted and configured by the player is a different learning ex-perience to the semantic ambiguity that may be present in a print-based play text. The world of a game such as *EverQuest*, in which the drama takes place, is constructed through an individual player's choices, which are unique for every player. Though there may be a high level of interpretation of meaning by the audience in a theatrical production, they cannot influence the outcome of the plot through their own actions. The interactive nature of the digital form is especially evident in video games but is also a characteristic of all currently evolving performance forms that rely on digital feedback either through mobile phones or the Internet. The situation is the same in any of the new interactive television forms: no audience participation, no show. This is clearly the case with television productions such as *Big Brother*, which depends on interactive viewers to drive the ongoing narrative of humiliation and eviction – not to mention the revenues it receives through premium text messages.

The underlying assumptions of live performance, even in mainstream theatre, have also moved to an acceptance of ambiguity in performance. The nature of character motivation may be deliberately unclear, as writers such as David Mamet emphasise in his work. Both his stage play *Oleanna* and his film *Wag the Dog* demonstrate levels of deliberate ambiguity as part of their appeal to the audience. However, within digital performance there is a further expectation by the audience that there will be multiple open narratives that can be manipulated to produce very different endings every time there is an audience or player interaction occurring.

The awareness of intertextuality and reference to other cultural and theatrical genres is also driving the production values of much current live performance. This self-referential nature and connection to the culturally commodified products of popular culture provides the common content that enables live performance to connect emotionally with its audience. In the field of digital performance the editing of video, hacking of game forms or textual poaching used to create new works is seen by the participants as the ultimate expression of the art form. For example, the appropriation of the video game *Halo* to produce a new digital drama, *Red vs Blue* has gained a cult status (www.redvsblue.com) with young audiences. The growth of the rap/scratch and MP3 download culture is a clear example of the trend in self-produced works. For many young people having to buy a commercial copy of a song or video is an admission of their failure as consumer/producers. It may be that much of intertextual layering of current *avant-garde* theatre is an attempt to connect to this new aesthetic of participation in a highly literate media audience.

Drama teachers who understand these emerging performance conventions can use them to engage their students as an audience for drama that explores authenticity and physical identity in new ways. They can also make use of the connection between the shifting conventions of live theatre as it accommodates itself to the evolving digital performance modes evolving around it. They will then be able to connect with their students and contemporary artistic representations of identity in a digital world of increasing image and text overload.

## Online drama and performance

Notions of performance and drama have been a popular theme in academic discussions of computers and cyberspace, see for example Murray (1997), Ryan, (1997) and Lanham (1993). These discussions characterise the digital medium as inherently playful and dramatic because of its interactivity and immersive quality, the release from physicality it offers and the rich array of easy-to-use possibilities at the user's disposal. The immersive quality of cyberspace is also described as removing the 'fourth wall', giving individuals a heightened feeling of participation, or a sense of being 'on stage rather than in the audience'. Computers and the online environment may be seen as creating a liminoid space, like that of theatre, offering a threshold experience in which we can temporarily escape reality.

This playfulness and theatricality may exist even in the more mundane everyday activities within the digital environment. As Barnes (2001, p239) comments, all online presentation is essentially performance-orientated. Even in text based communication, the traditional use of language is altered, creating visually orientated playful text in which '...participants appear to be engaging in a mode of writing which resembles a theatrical performance'. Danet (2001) also describes this kind of textual play, particularly in forms of online chat, which she suggests involve a kind of spontaneous, improvised performance akin to jazz.

This digital environment may also be employed as an overtly theatrical space. As Murray (1997, p125) comments, '...the computer is providing us with a new stage for the creation of participatory theatre.' Forms of online performance differ from conventional notions of theatre in that they are distanced from the physical body. Some writers have suggested that this distance frees people even further to experiment with different ways of being. For instance, LaFarge (1995, p415-422) argues that the anonymity afforded by the virtual environment allows for much more adventurous performance and a psychologically richer experience.

One recent development has been in Multiplayer Online Games (MOG) like *EverQuest* with at its peak over 100,000 role-based performers simultaneously interacting within the one online environment. As well as role-playing games, virtual worlds such as Linden Labs' *Second Life* (http:// secondlife.com) allow users great flexibility to create tools and services and even to manipulate the physics of their virtual space. As Sherry Turkle (1997, p11) points out, game players are game authors, creators as well as consumers of the media content. In this sense, participating in a multiplayer online environment also has much in common with '...script writing, performance art, street theatre, improvisational theatre-or even *commedia dell arte*'.

In this space, the boundaries between author and spectator, actor and character are blurred. Individuals involved in these interactive environments are required to engage in a kind of improvised performance. But computer/ video games differ from true improvisation in that in the game pretext, the world of probabilities inherent in the game, is predetermined. It is not possible for players to think outside the box: it is improvised performance within a sequence of loosely narrative situations and events that the player can choose to interact with or not. Nevertheless this is very different from possible responses to a scripted play or film.

For Murray (1997, p44) this improvised performance can be seen as creating a collective narrative. As she writes '...this new kind of adult narrative pleasure involves the sustained collaborative writing of stories that are mixtures of the narrated and the dramatised'. However, interactivity may not necessarily be compatible with the traditional notion of narrative, as we discuss later.

### Play and improvisational performance

Because of this level of interactivity and lack of semantic depth, it has been argued that narrative on its own is simply not adequate for the analysis of interactive digital media. Instead, the improvised nature of game narrative and the necessary repetition required to complete the story suggests that something other than the pleasure of traditional storytelling is going on. As Murray (1997, p88) points out, stories only require that we pay attention, whilst games involve activity and are focused on gaining a skill. Process drama, however, requires attention, role commitment and interaction.

### Performing identity

The notion of identity formation within the digital/virtual environment has been a dominant theme in studies of cyberculture, particularly in the way the presentation of the self in the online environment may obfuscate and challenge traditional notions of identity, especially in the context of race, class, gender and sexuality.

These cybercultural studies reflect post-structural notions of identity that challenge the Cartesian notion of the essential self: that we are born with a fixed and stable identity. Instead, social constructionist conceptions of identity involve a decentring of the self which emphasises the spatial and temporal locatedness of identity. Rather than being fixed, identities are seen as 'necessary fictions' or 'points of temporary attachment to the subject positions which discursive practices construct for us' (Hall, 2000, p1-17).

This challenge to essentialist notions of the fixed self also opens up possibilities for reconstructing identity. For example, in his book *Modernity and Self Identity* (1991) Anthony Giddens addresses the idea of identity as a project. In Giddens' work and that of Ulrich Beck (1992) the breakdown of traditional cultural markers, the globalisation of late modern society and the consequent disembedding of the self has led to less fixed notions of identity. As a result, in contemporary society, biography and identity may be less fixed and more open than it was in the past. As Giddens suggests, the self becomes a reflexive project in which decisions concerning lifestyle 'give material form to a particular narrative self-identity'(Giddens, 1991, p47). This ongoing reflexive project of self-identity involves sustaining a 'coherent, yet continuously revised, biographical narrative' (Giddens, 1991, p6).

This is of particular interest in the context of the reflexivity and choice involved in the self-presentation of online identities. One example is the self-reflexive construction of identity on personal Web pages. As Cheung (2000, p45) writes, '...using the expressive resources of the personal homepage, authors can choose which aspects of their multiple and contradictory selves they wish to present.' The *self* or *selves* presented on personal homepages are highly contrived artefacts since homepage authors consciously select particular parts of their selves for presentation.

This freedom to experiment with identity is even more evident in text-based environments such as chat rooms and blogs 'where the self is multiple and constructed through language ' (Turkle, 1995, p184). As Bell (2001, p116) suggests, '...if we type ourselves into being in cyberspace... we can make and re-make who we are endlessly, liberated from the 'meat' of our RL (Real Life) bodies and all the identity-markers they carry.'

This kind of self-presentation is highly performative. As Nakamura says (2000, p713), individuals are required to '...project a version of the self which is inherently theatrical'. It could also be argued that what happens in the performance of gender identities online highlights the way in which all gender is performative. There is no doubt that gender role-play occupies a lot of text-based interaction online!

This argument suggests that the anonymity of cyberspace gives people the chance to express multiple and often unexplored aspects of the self, to play with their identity and to try out new ones. In this context a number of writers have commented on the similarity between the liminoid space of cyberspace and the Bakhtinian notion of carnival, for instance in the way in which the anonymity, or pseudonymity, offered by online interaction hides identity and reduces accountability '...as efficiently as the all-enveloping costumes and masks worn at carnival time' (Danet, 2001, p8). Just as disguised individuals in carnival may enjoy reduced accountability and the freedom to express themselves in ways which might be unacceptable within the sphere of everyday life, so the anonymity of cyberspace may open new possibilities for exploring alternate identities, as the following cartoon makes clear.

**Figure 2.1: Peter Steiner's famous cartoon from**
***The New Yorker,* (Vol.69 (LXIX) no. 20) July 5, 1993, p61**

*"On the Internet, nobody knows you're a dog."*

## Beyond narrative

Manovitch (1999, p173) comments on the need to look beyond narrative in the context of the digital performance. As he suggests

> ...as exciting as the ideas of a viewer participating in the story, choosing different paths through the narrative space, and interacting with characters may be, they address only one aspect of cinema that is neither unique nor, as many will argue, essential to it: narrative.

When almost everything can be simulated in the computer, filming physical reality becomes just one possibility, challenging the dominant *genre* of film as fictional live-action films: the largely unmodified lens-based recording of events in real physical space. Manovitch (1999) argues that the ability to create digitised photorealistic images, which have never been 'filmed', has the potential to displace live action footage from its privileged role as the only source of cinematic material. Once live action is digitised, it is reduced to one among many graphics that can be manipulated, becoming the raw material for further composition. Thus shot footage is no longer the final point, but rather the first stage of post-production. Already there are examples of photo-realistic live footage in movies such as the recent *Final Fantasy*.

On a more technical level new digital technology offers performers new ways of engaging with texts. For instance, as well as accessing archives on the net, technology like DVDs create the potential to search content and actively manipulate the viewing experience, offering a far more sophisticated method of doing what was once achieved with the fast forward button. In addition, increasing lay expertise with digital technologies creates new possibilities for textual poaching through which viewers actively appropriate, manipulate and reinvent narrative, becoming textual producers rather than just consumers.

Ask young people about the dramatic performances they value at the moment. Online role-playing games like *EverQuest*, and *World of Warcraft* with millions of players worldwide are starting to take over from the imagined reality of the digitally constructed worlds in films like *The Matrix* and *The Terminator*.

## Drama teachers and technology

Maybe it is only drama teachers inside the school community who really understand what this shift in perception means and can provide the role-based performance space for an explanation and critique of current cultural practices.

By providing role protection and role distance through drama and physical theatre teachers can help provide the emotional literacy required for their students in a way that is not catered for in other areas of the curriculum. An adaptation of the drama conventions outlined by Jonathan Neelands and Tony Goode (2000) for use with the digital technologies of the mobile phone and the Internet seems a good place to start. Another useful approach we discuss is to set up a drama pretext using Webpage resources as a starting place for drama.

So move over Arnold Schwarzenegger and the clunky cyborgs of the past. Digital performance is already being created in the minds and computers of young online performers, enhanced by digital imaging. It's going to produce some interesting notions of what constitutes dramatic performances in the future. In the next chapter we discuss the implications of teaching these evolving dramatic forms in contemporary drama classrooms.

# 3
## The challenges of the digital generation

### The brave new world?

The vision that seemed to fill educational planners with joy and teachers with dread was the naive view that soon students would be walking into teacher-free classrooms and interacting with an electronic box of some sort. Rows of smiling children would peer into computer screens where they could learn everything they needed to learn. No need for any human interaction at all. How cost effective! How rational!

This is the magic pill model of education, where all your needs for food and drink can be contained within some sort of nutritional supplement. What those who propagate the teacher-less classroom and the magic pill forgot is that the experience, the live interaction is central to both learning and dining. The pill, while it may pragmatically fill a need for supplementary nutrition, does not provide the experience of a carefully prepared dish or a full smooth and rich red wine in the company of friends and family. The proponents of the classroom of the future misunderstood that teaching and learning is often about the human interaction, the experience and the liveness of the interaction.

This chapter looks at the challenge of teaching in the drama classroom of the future. It examines the present generation of teachers and students and assesses the perceived or real chasm that exists between them, then examines some of the existing and emerging kinds of technology available for drama learning that can reinforce the community of practice model and the digital interactivity of the drama classroom. The chapter concludes with a discussion of how the aesthetics of drama education may need to be reformed to use the creative potential of technology for teachers and students in drama learning.

## Teachers and technology

Non-teachers often push 'radical technological change' as the way towards alleviating perceived educational shortcomings (Cuban, 1986). Teachers are often resolutely and justifiably resistant to classroom tools that undermine rather than enhance the learning experience of their students. When teachers have rejected these magic pills they often feel the wrath of those boosting the technology. Cuban argues that the magic pill approach to fixing educational problems with technology leads to a cycle of blame where teachers are ultimately scapegoated for being stubborn or intransient. At this point in the cycle after experts have mandated technological use after dubious surveys, educators are vilified with stinging rebukes and characterised as:

> ...narrow-minded, stubborn teachers reluctant to use learning tools that had been shown to be academically effective. Once limited classroom use had been established, teacher-bashing... produced a series of sharp critiques blaming intransigent teachers for blocking improvements through modern technology. Few scholars, policy makers, or practitioners ever questioned the claims of boosters or even asked whether technology should be introduced. (Cuban, 1986, p5)

If you walk into drama classrooms today you will see that not much has changed in the last fifteen years. The lighting bar may have some new lights and there may be a computer up the back but not that much has changed despite the amazing revolution in digital technology. There are many reasons why this is so across education in general. There is no doubt that there has been an uneven, *ad hoc* approach to technology provision in many school systems promoted by some who are more interested in profit rather than education.

We are not blaming teachers for the slow uptake of technology. Although there is evidence of resistance to the introduction and implementation of technology (Flintoff, 2002a; Knezek and Christensen, 2002), it does not necessarily follow that teachers are blocking sensible progress. More likely teachers are reluctant to introduce technology not because they are luddites, but because a compelling case has not been mounted for the introduction of assorted technologies. The rest of this chapter discusses ways that drama educators might engage with such technology in their classrooms.

As drama teachers know, no number of textbooks, technical wizardry or computer programmes can provide the live experience of performance in the classroom. You cannot understand Heathcote's 'living through' drama unless you actually live the experience. The simplicity and power of the live interaction in the empty space is an essential feature of drama education. Peter Brook famously nominated interaction with the live actor in the empty space as the essence of the drama aesthetic: 'A man walks across this empty space whilst someone else is watching him, and this is all that is needed for an actor of theatre to be engaged' (Brook, 1980, p9).

Theatre and drama teaching is about experiencing the wonder of the live actor in the live space. However, the perception of what is live in a mediatised culture is a central issue. Technology has radically influenced the concept of *liveness* within all forms of dramatic performance. Far from dehumanising and debasing that experience, technology can support the evolving perception of liveness in drama teaching. Young people are digital natives: they grow up using digital technologies in every part of their lives. More and more young people use technology as a stage on which they can explore their creativity. If drama educators ignore this generation's fluency in technology they may miss exciting classroom possibilities.

Haseman (2004) claims that drama teachers are ideally suited to the challenges presented by digital natives. He says that drama educators can '...position themselves with the most engaging pedagogy for this new age. We need to connect our classrooms and studios so the creative and research possibilities of digital technologies can be powerfully linked with our distinctive pedagogy' (p 22).

The drama classroom should not be made post-human: on the contrary technology can be used in drama to put the human experience at the centre of learning. If drama teachers explore this emerging space in real and virtual worlds, there is enormous scope for renewed creative experiences in the drama classroom. There is also significant pressure from the community, government and schooling systems to speed this integration of contemporary technologies into the school system.

## The technology push

At a school systems level authorities and educational policy bodies in Australia and the United Kingdom and elsewhere are mandating integration of Information and Communications Technology (ICT) in to the drama curriculum. Recently the New South Wales[1] (Australia) Board of Studies[2] mandated

ICT as an area of cross curriculum content necessitating its inclusion in all Years 7-10 syllabi which includes all of the arts. The Year 7-10 drama syllabus (BOS, 2003, p15) says, '...teachers should allow students the opportunity to explore different information communication technologies in their class work'. This system proscription severely underestimates the serious real world classroom issues of integrating technologies into learning unless there is a conceptual framework to provide direction.

## E-learning with digital natives

Simply shifting traditional learning materials to a computer is no guarantee that learning will improve or will even occur. Shepherd (2001, para 2) argues that e-learning methods, like other more traditional teaching methods, can be passive and sterile: '...in other words, they're just plain dull, and dull won't hack it with a generation reared on techno music, action movies and video games'. He argues that computer games and simulations offer the opportunity to provide an engaging learner experience that builds real skills, but within a protected and supported learning environment. Squire and Jenkins (2004, p8) explain the chasm that has opened up between the multi-million dollar game titles that are developed and the meagre resources used to develop education projects. There is a magnificent potential for engagement and learning through games, but as Squire and Jenkins argue:

> Few educational games keep pace with contemporary entertainment titles and thus fail to achieve this potential. Frankly, most existing edutainment products combine the entertainment value of a bad lecture with the educational value of a bad game.

As this chasm widens we have a new generation of digital natives who see the digital world as normal and as an integral part of their lives.

## Teaching the aliens in the classroom

As we have discussed Prensky's *Digital Game-Based Learning* (2001a) suggests that educators must soon deal with the *games generation* – which he labels *digital natives*. He argues that people under the age of 30 have grown up with digital technology and are proficient with its applications. As most teachers are older than their students there is a generational/technological chasm emerging between teachers and learners.

*Digital Game-Based Learning* describes a teaching framework (Prensky, 2001a, p3) with the following features:

- a melding of education and interactive entertainment to meet the needs and learning styles of new generations of learners
- material that will motivate because it is fun
- adaptability and effectiveness for all learning needs.

Green and Bigum (1993) suggest that new technologies, especially computer and video games, have impacted so greatly on young people that many teachers feel they are now confronted by 'aliens in the classroom'. Katz (2000) argues that new forms of popular culture, mostly involving computers, have developed so quickly that there has evolved '...perhaps the widest gap – informational, cultural and factual-between the young and the old in human history'. He argues that while many adults insist they have lessons to teach the next generation, all they have to offer are boring and outmoded educational systems. Both Katz and Prensky use the image of a chasm to illustrate this generational divide. Katz (2000) places gaming at the 'centre of this chasm': extending the gap between the generations. Prensky (2001b) sees video and computer games as a bridge across the gap, allowing better communication between generations.

Prensky argues that this generational chasm manifests itself in ten basic cognitive changes apparent in the games generation. Many of these changes are already well understood and catered for by drama educators. The potential implications for learning and teaching in traditional classrooms is outlined in Table 3.1 on page 42.

Fromme (2001, p2) agrees that this generational shift is dramatic. He argues that '...parents and teachers tend to address the media cultures of the younger from their own generational perspective' while they ignore the digital media literacy of children and young adults. There are potential obstacles to learning that may arise from the use of teaching methods that do not account for generational differences in changing media cultures. Educators '...ignore or slight the Nintendo generation, or indeed demonise them, at their own peril' (Green, Reid and Bigum, 1998).

Digital game-based learning does not simply mean using video games in a classroom environment – though that may be part of an overall strategy – but describes the blending of digital technology (computers, multimedia, online) with an interactive drama activity that accesses the knowledge of communities of practice, that is engaging and that produces a learning outcome. That was the approach taken with the *Flood* and the *To the Spice Islands* projects described in Chapter 6. It is the focus of epistemic games and is at

**Table 3.1: Ten learning preferences of Prensky's 'Digital Natives' (from Prensky, 2001a, 2001b)**

| Digital natives prefer: | Traditional teaching provides: | Learning implications: |
| --- | --- | --- |
| 1 'Twitch' speed | Conventional speed | Students desire faster interaction with information (game speed) |
| 2 Parallel processing | Linear processing | Students desire multitasking, processing multiple data simultaneously |
| 3 Graphics first | Text first | Students desire graphic information with a text backup |
| 4 Random access | Step-by-step | Students prefer hyperlinking through materials, rather than reading from beginning to end |
| 5 Connectivity | Stand alone | Students prefer networking, and high level of electronic communication |
| 6 Activity | Passivity | Less tolerance for passive instructional situations-learn by doing |
| 7 Play | Work | Students see computers as toys as well as tools; prefer to learn in a fun environment |
| 8 Payoff | Patience | Expect immediate and clear feedback or reward in return for efforts |
| 9 Fantasy | Reality | Fantasy and play elements are an accepted part of 'serious' work, e.g. informal work settings |
| 10 Technology-as-friend | Technology-as-foe | See technology as empowering and necessary |

the centre of the serious games movement. But there are some important funding and resource implications for this curriculum change.

## Resources and the digital world

Leyland (1996) notes that the use of technology to engage students can lie outside the means or budget of educators, resulting in a gap between expectations and resources. The cost of technology contributes to reservations about the use of video games in the classroom (Smith, Curtin and Newman, 1997), such that even pro-technology teachers rely on imagination rather than multimedia tools to engage their students. Prensky (2001a, p357) glibly describes the potential price range of training software: 'how much does digital game-based learning cost? The answer is an easy one – between $300 and $3 million'. Some game solutions can be cheap, even free, but the development costs of high-end educational materials can be the equivalent of big budget commercial game projects. Prensky's pitch is clearly aimed at a corporate environment with large training budgets. Projects such as the *Flood* and *To the Spice Islands* demonstrate that the digital game-based learning approach is not entirely beyond the reach of the modestly financed end of education and training and that drama educators have some experience in embracing technology.

## Drama teachers and technology

In a recent study into teachers' attitudes toward technology Knezek and Christensen (2002, p375) found that when teachers used and were supported in the use of the technology they felt more positive about using it in their classrooms. This was based on effective needs-based training relating directly to their teaching areas. By contrast, other training with general rather than specific application to curriculum areas was not as successful. Recent research (Anderson, 2002) found that resistance to technology was the result of inadequate and irrelevant training. One of the primary drama educators recalls her experience:

> Recently I did a course that was supposed to help teachers understand technology. It was my idea of hell. I used to fall asleep it was so boring. The presenters were all inspired with all this knowledge to impart but everyone else could barely focus. The presenter at the course was boring, did not know what was happening and did not have control over the knowledge she was supposed to be imparting. It was poorly and hastily organised. The technology training was poor because it ignored teachers' situations and needs (Anderson, 2002, p142).

Drama educators have demonstrated mixed rates of participation and enthusiasm for the introduction of everyday technology in their classrooms. In an Australian study half the respondents surveyed were not using digital technology of any kind in their drama classes (Flintoff, 2002b). A recently completed survey by the British Office for Standards in Education (Ofsted) found that Information Communication Technology (ICT) use in drama classes was unsatisfactory in 10 per cent of cases and only satisfactory in 50 per cent of classrooms. Ofsted concluded from these results that in drama classrooms '...too little use is made of ICT...' (Ofsted, 2004). Some teachers reported that the use of technology dehumanised or disembodied drama (Flintoff, 2002a).

This attitude reflects the dichotomies in the dramatic arts that Auslander identifies between the valorised live performance forms and the dehumanised, disembodied mediatised form (1999, p1). The apparent irony is that while some teachers are unconvinced of or resistant to the integration of ICT and drama, their students are engaging in and consuming technology in ever increasing numbers (Australian Bureau of Statistics, 2004). Much of this participation or immersion is in the same activities that take place in a performing arts classroom, such as role-based games.

## The challenge of technology and drama education

The prevalence of and pressure for integration of new technologies in the drama classroom is also challenging drama educators to incorporate technology into their teaching. The ubiquity of technology that relates to drama education is facing teachers with serious challenges to engage with a dramatic aesthetic in classrooms. Perhaps the most immediate challenge is the exposure and experience today's children have to rapidly changing technologies. Morris (2004) argues that students are less familiar with traditional theatre as they are immersed in mediatised drama forms. Her justifiable claim is that the '...experience of drama is less likely to be through live performance than through screen-based media such as television, film, videos, video games, CD-Rom, DVD-ROM and interactive Web-based games' (2004, p134). Australian national statistics (ABS, 2002) support this trend. In 2002, 70 per cent of the population saw a film and 18 per cent attended a theatrical performance. In the same period in the UK 61 per cent went to the cinema and 24 per cent to a play (National Statistics, 2004).

There are real and compelling challenges in implementing technology in the drama classroom, ranging from resources to the inadequacy of the training. The consequences of not engaging are also profound. Our digital native students are using, consuming and producing digital content at an ever increasing pace. If drama educators do not provide ways for them to engage with drama using technologies they may go elsewhere. Thankfully there are resources already available and being developed which will assist drama teachers to use technologies in their practice.

A brief survey of available computer-based technology falls into three general categories. Apart from instrumental tool-based computer applications, such as design or video editing packages, there are specific kinds of technology to assist in teaching drama. These fall broadly into the categories of drama teaching resources, simulations and games. The following section examines some of these resources.

## Drama teaching resources

Teachers, curriculum designers and academics in drama education have responded in diverse ways to the constraints and possibilities offered by technology. More recent drama and technology resources have addressed the issues directly relating to the aesthetics of drama and technology. Readman and Wise (2004) developed a CD- ROM exploring a physical theatre production through performance highlights, visual, aural and textual pretexts, teaching units, live Web links and interviews. This CD complements many of the drama processes already used in drama classrooms and presents ways for technology to support them. The CD-ROM, *Physical Theatre Performance and Pretext* follows the development of a physical theatre performance and develops a series of resources around the devising process. The designers include the following theorists' work as central to their own work (Readman and Wise, 2004, p93):

- Neelands' (2004) description of a para-aesthetic approach
- Boal's (1979) desire to influence reality not merely reflect it
- Friere's (1985) urge to identify the transformative purpose of education and see it as a humanistic and liberating task and
- McLean's (1996) and Abbs' (1987) research into the aesthetic, link the broader philosophies of aesthetics to the pedagogical practice central to this design.

The significance of this aesthetic positioning lies not in its content, which is also significant, but in the actual consideration of how technology, aesthetics and drama education interrelate. This welcome development recognises that curriculum and resource designers will have to work differently to understand and teach in the digital drama classrooms of the future. The designers of this CD-ROM position themselves squarely within the aesthetic orthodoxy

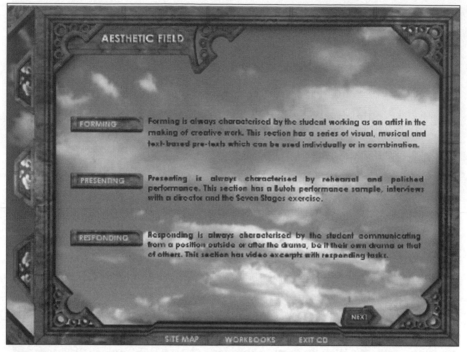

**Figure 3.1: A screenshot from Physical Theatre Performance and Pretext**

of drama education but claim links from the 'virtual' to real and transcendent experience so often claimed for drama education and theatre practice. In essence they have adapted the aesthetics of drama education in a live sense to the computer-mediated world. The frame from the CD-ROM shown in Figure 3.1 demonstrates their engagement with the aesthetics of drama education.

## Drama simulations

*StageStruck* is a CD-ROM package developed by Australia's National Institute of Dramatic Art (NIDA) in 1998. The package allows the user to direct and design a computer-based performance. It is a pioneering resource offering students the opportunity to devise virtual performances, including creating blocking, stage design, sound design and limited scriptwrighting from a database of movement, sound and dialogue. The designers of *StageStruck* have developed a simulation that provides an engagement with: '...more realistic, complex issues associated with directing and delivering a performance. Students are able to immerse themselves in the world of performance'. The resource gives students a first-hand experience of: '... stage depth, a rich sound accompaniment and effective, realistic animated performer move-

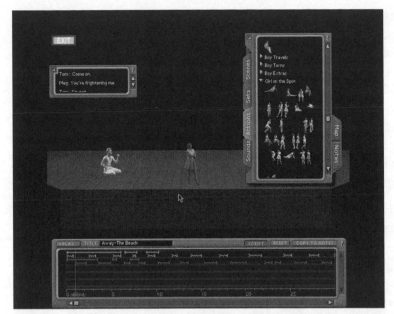

**Figure 3.2: A screenshot from *StageStruck* demonstrating the student's control of characters, actions and dialogue**

ments ... a variety of video-based animations of recorded movement...'
(Wright, Hedberg, and Harper, 1998, p674). Most importantly, the resource
demonstrates the different intentions directors and actors bring to text. 'The
user can identify the actor's intention behind making a movement or saying
a line and this is used as the basis for selecting the recorded movement or
speech' (Wright, Hedberg, and Harper, 1998, p674). Beyond understanding
and identifying intention students can create their own. The challenge, as
always, is to transfer those skills to students' own performance-making.

*StageStruck* attempts to recreate the action of the theatre for students and it
provides an evocative understanding of the theatre for younger students. It
was never intended to replace the experience of participation in the theatre.
Amanda Morris, one of the chief designers, argues that the resource is useless
without the dramatic skills and understanding of teachers and students. Far
from teaching being replaced by technology she argues that

> ...technology is only equipment and processes that allow you and you and
> your students to explore drama in an exciting way. Your students' ideas and
> their skill in creatively shaping these into dramatic experiences are the most
> important aspect of drama in the classroom. Technology is there to enhance
> and extend this experience, not replace it. (Morris, 2004, p147)

## Playing games

The playfulness inherent in drama education would seem a strong match to the world of digital gaming. Drama educators are familiar with the creation of new worlds, the taking on of roles and the development of societies. There are several popular programmes such as *The Sims* and *Civilization* that do just that, provide roles and give participants the experience of living as another. Drama educators would see this as a kind of metaxis[3] (Boal, 1995, p43) where we are aware of our own reality and create other characters and worlds through our own reality. Currently there are at least two games in development that have the potential to create drama in real and virtual spaces.

*Prospero's Island* is being developed jointly between Massachusetts Institute of Technology (MIT) and the Royal Shakespeare Company (RSC). The single player game anticipates the creation of literary works that look more like games (Squire and Jenkins, 2004). *Prospero's Island* is an exploration of the themes and plot and arise from the theatricality of the performance by the Royal Shakespeare Company. The creators have devised the work as a single player game that can be played by students at home and then brought into a drama or English class as an object for analysis. The player chooses costumes, which in turn selects their role. The player then interacts with the characters of *The Tempest*, such as Caliban and Ariel, and create their own version of Shakespeare's play. Squire and Jenkins (2004, p21) argue that *Prospero's Island* is a space for:

> ...dreams and magic, and students are encouraged to decipher symbols, manipulate language, and uncover secrets (in short to perform literary analysis)... *Prospero's Island* encourages students to experience the plays not simply as readers or spectators but as players, directors and authors. As students become immersed in this world, they learn more about the play, they experience embodiments of central metaphors in the text they master the core characters' desires and relationships, and they learn about the role magic and dreams play in the Renaissance imagination. Yet, they also learn something about themselves, the choices they make, the identities they play, and the ways they are seen by other people – issues that are central to the experience of adolescence.

Compare this with an analysis of an unrelated process drama. Margery Hertzberg (2003) created a process drama with a group of 10 and 11 year old students. This work was designed to investigate how process drama could deepen the experience and engagement of reading a novel:

> The power of metaxis through enactment that aids in connecting the real world to the fiction of the book is the unique quality that process drama can

bring to a critical reading of a text. By making personal connections to events in the book, children can more deeply explore issues both within and beyond their immediate lives...Children can debate and challenge their own thoughts and the thoughts of others from an 'as if' stance. As one child said after participating in the drama activity, 'They might be being bullied in the story and the same thing's happening to you, so there's a link between reality and fiction.'

Hertzberg's description has marked similarities with the world of the game. The playfulness and the ability for the player to be themselves and another character at the same time provide commonalities with the process drama. Some may argue that this kind of approach to literature has the tendency to trivialise; that making *The Tempest* into a game reduces the gravitas and the greatness of the writing. It might be criticised as being an attempt to replace the play with a dumbed down version. Squire and Jenkins argue that, on the contrary, it will enrich and extend the experience for students:

> In the end, should the student go from playing the game to watching a performance of *The Tempest*, she will be in roughly the position of an original spectator at the Globe – she will know some aspects of the story, be familiar with the world in which it is set, have some access to the information on which its central metaphors operate, and perhaps be able to more fully enjoy the immediate experience of the performance. The game does not displace the play. Rather, game playing enhances the experience of watching the play, much the way students reading part of the text aloud or enacting scenes in their classrooms historically has. (2004, p22)

There is in the game and the process drama an inherent playfulness, exploration, self-discovery and links to the imagination. In both cases there is an attempt to provide a deep understanding of literature. *Prospero's Island* creates an online process drama that can deepen the experience of the play and unleash the imagination of the student-actor in the piece. Rather than just surface reading, participants in the game and the process drama get to 'embody' virtually and in real spaces the text of the literature in greater depth.

If teachers and students are to introduce these approaches into their drama, how might teachers need to rethink what they do in drama education? What will happen to the way we think about drama if we embrace technology? Will the central aesthetics of drama education shift?

## Playing upon new 'stages': technology and drama education aesthetics

Aesthetics is a slippery and problematic term for many drama educators, as Jackson has pointed out (1999, p51). For us aesthetics is the quality of the artistic experience for the participant and the observer. We share Jackson's view that the aesthetic is not necessarily about refinement or high art or even beauty. While those may be features of a drama education classroom, aesthetics are more about the quality of the engagement on the stage or in the classroom. Jackson is speaking here about Theatre in Education but the same process is at work in drama learning in the classroom and beyond:

> ...far from being diversionary, elitist or secondary to the 'real' business of what the play is about is actually central to the effectiveness of educational theatre; that the aesthetic dimension must form a serious evaluation of the educational experience of young audiences. (1999, p51)

The wide-scale introduction of digital technology has transformed aesthetics in many areas. The advances in editing and presentation technologies have transformed film, television and digital media aesthetics. Theatre itself has been changed and will continue to change with the introduction of many new aesthetic features. Those interested in the health of theatre as a dynamic and changing art form will surely be cheering on these changes.

Drama education changes in response to all kinds of influences, including technology. A role-based scenario online has different aesthetic properties from a role-based drama in real time in a real space. A performance developed through an online pretext may differ from that developed from a written pretext. An exploration of a dramatic scenario online with characters has different features but that does not make the experience less valid. It is the students and teachers who have the strongest influence over the success of the aesthetic experience. The quality of the aesthetic experience relies most heavily on the creative skills of the dramatist – in this case the teachers and students – rather than the choice of medium.

The irony is that teachers whose stock in trade is the imagined and the virtual are sometimes resistant to that same world when it becomes disembodied on a screen (Carroll, 2002). Other art forms such as visual arts and music seem to have little difficulty in accepting that the introduction of technology will not mean the new forms are of lesser value; they simply constitute a different aesthetic experience and response. Visual arts demand several different sets of skills and understandings to develop works: the skills of a sculptor differ from those of a digital artist. While these skills and understandings may be founded in a common understanding of the aesthetics of visual arts the medium is important in the development of the artistic work.

This approach has not been as readily accepted by drama educators. How can a shift in thinking be achieved so they can see that drama happens in all sorts of media for all sorts of dramatic intentions? To deny the multiple stages on which drama is played is to limit the potential for student creativity and the strength of the art form to adapt to many media and communicate authentically. Dramatic meaning can be powerfully expressed on screens, stages or on platforms that have not even been invented yet; such is the power of the art form. The dramatic property may be developed for the live stage but could be made into an online game or a short story or a digital art work. All these forms have their own aesthetic forms and conventions which the student must understand to explore these other stages. The drama educator has a significant role here. But before discussing the conventions of other stages we should examine how the aesthetics of drama education might be changed in response to technology and what might constitute a drama education aesthetic for the 21st Century.

## Reviewing the aesthetics of drama education

This resetting and reconceptualising of aesthetic features is designed to 're-fence' (Haseman, 2004, p19) the field of contemporary drama to include the media used for drama but which have only recently been recognised as potential stages for drama. The table on page 52 outlines McLean's (1996) 'possible definition' of drama aesthetics and proposes the new aesthetic framework incorporating ICT with the features of each indicated.

Judith McLean's discussion of aesthetics in drama was an important step in the development of understanding this area. This framework updates her initial pioneering work in the light of the recent advances in technology.

The assumption in her definition is of a live aesthetic engagement: she talks about 'curriculum based' drama carried out in 'everyday classrooms' (McLean, 1996, p8). McLean nominates three conditions that should be present for the drama aesthetic to occur (McLean, 1996, p14):

■ The importance of dialogue

■ The importance of experiential learning and teacher/students working as co-artists

■ The importance of critical reflection.

**Table 3.2: Framework for drama aesthetics**

| A possible understanding of aesthetics (McLean, 1996) | Features | Integrating technology and drama aesthetics | Features |
|---|---|---|---|
| The importance of dialogue | • Focuses on shared experiences<br>• Emphasises the importance of presence<br>• Is often linear in approach | • The importance of interactivity | • Experiences are shared but not necessarily at the same time<br>• Not necessarily linear<br>• Less focus on the physical and more on the imaginative |
| The importance of experiential learning and teacher/students working as co-artists | • Emphasises the experience in real time<br>• Focuses on teachers and students working as co-artists<br>• Complex relationship between teacher and student as the initiator and controller of form and ideas | • Experiential learning can occur virtually<br>• Relationship between teacher and student made more complex as students are often the experts in the technology | • Roles are not bound by physical constraints (gender, physical attributes) |
| The importance of critical reflection | • Respect and validating student voices | • The importance of online protocols and forms | • Developing a critical awareness of computer based technologies as a tool for dramatic experiences |

## The importance of dialogue

This definition prioritises presence and dialogue 'in the drama classroom' (McLean, 1996, p14). This works to the exclusion of virtual forms of drama and restricts the medium to the live classroom or stage. Instead of seeing drama as solely the domain of the live stage, we argue drama can and does happen on stage, on screen, in real and virtual spaces and in a mixture of all of these. Presence should be enlarged to include the possibility that the 'actors' are present in the drama but not necessarily present in the same space or at the same time. This may seem like a fine distinction but the online world will allow players or actors to be present with each other in a drama or a game without actually being in the same space. For instance in the *To The Spice Islands* project referred to in Chapter 6 students, teachers and Web designers are shown participating in a process drama in different places at different times. These digital native students had little difficulty working upon digital and live stages simultaneously.

A more mainstream example is found in the simulation games such as *World of Warcraft* and *Battlefield 1942* being played in cyberspace by virtual armies of young as well as not so young people. Janet Murray (1997, p208) defines these games as cyberdrama if they give human participants agency, immersion and the possibility of transformation. Most drama teachers aim to give their students such opportunities in their drama classroom experiences.

Games such as *Zork, EverQuest* and *The Sims* have elements in them of cyberdrama (Wardrip-Fruin, 2004, p1). Even though all the participants are not present they are still engaged in the drama and working collaboratively and interactively. In this sense the drama is working on students being present but not all at the same time or in the same space. The dialogue is created and developed but in an asynchronous fashion.

The body is present but virtual, as is the dialogue. Without seeing the body you have fewer barriers to creating what the student imagines (Carroll, 2004, p72). This does have important implications for managing the drama and is the source of resistance from some teachers to this form of dramatic expression. Flintoff (2002a, p194) argues that the body is still present but in a different position from drama in real spaces. This changes the aesthetic but allows us to enrich the aesthetic experience online. Instead of seeing technology as a threat to drama, it is useful to consider how drama might influence, change and improve technology. How can drama create the authentic online? How can drama create an awareness of others? According to Murray (1997), it already has and does in its ability to engage and immerse participants in each other's virtual worlds.

## The importance of experiential learning and teacher/students working as co-artists

McLean nominates experiential learning as the next essential to the aesthetic occurring in the classroom. In her analysis, experiential learning takes place as the student and teacher engage in a complex collaboration between form and ideas. This is the human interaction also apparent in digital dramas and especially in *Project Woomera* developed at Queensland University of Technology. In this drama, coordinated by Brad Haseman and Kim Flintoff, students were involved in a real-time online role-play that asked them to board the spaceship Woomera to solve an 'urgent environmental problem'. What evolved was 'an exploration of human rights, mandatory detention, social tolerance, prejudice, religious intolerance and personal dilemma' (Flintoff, 2002b, p6). For these students the learning was experiential and situated within a simulated community of practice (Wegner, 1998) – in this case prison wardens. The learning which takes place is sometimes mediated through the game but, like Heathcote's Commission Model and serious games discussed in Chapter 1, an attempt is made to understand the depth and breadth of the issue by working as a community. These students were involved in authentic experiential workshops, only the stage or platform changed. Instead of being in a real classroom the dramatic experience occurred online.

One of the bases of the drama aesthetic, the centrality of experiential learning, is not debased through being online although it is changed. In these online dramas, as in traditional classroom dramas, systems and roles are created for students to experience alternative worlds. The difference with the online world is that they are created in virtual rather than real spaces. This jump from real to virtual space does not dilute the experience; it changes the nature of it. Dorothy Heathcote's approach to the development of virtual communities of practice reflects many of the online drama projects being developed today. Heathcote says of her dramas: '...all the work of drama is about cultures and communities and about group systems' (Heathcote, 1984, p25). She defines drama unequivocally as an 'art' that depends on the creation of cultures and communities. *Project Woomera* created a similar kind of world where students engage with each other and with teacher-artists to examine the results of conflict generated by the drama whether it is online or in real classroom space. This would be a fitting description of many of the games available today, including *The Sims* and *EverQuest*.

A growing sense of community is also emerging amongst game players as there is in the process drama approach. While it is true that many games are played by one person only, there are also many that rely on teamwork. Currently a game called *Revolution* at MIT is being developed that involves multiple players in a multiplayer online role-playing game set during the American War for Independence. Coincidentally, Taylor (1998) approaches the very same topic with the same aims (p62), immersing his students through the power of process drama in a seminal moment of American history as a collaborative exercise. In this comparison both process drama and online gaming are being used to simulate the same historical event to encourage an immersive learning experience. Although the space may change from classroom to online, the aims of immersion, collaboration and deepened understanding are the same in process dramas and team-oriented epistemic games.

### The importance of critical reflection

The advent of an overwhelming volume of knowledge has heightened the importance of critical engagement in education but particularly within drama education. McLean's inclusion of critical reflection asks students to examine what they have before them and returns participants to one of the central questions in drama learning: '...is this authentic?' (Bolton, 1998, p244). Heathcote's Commission Model (2003) further interrogates authenticity by giving participants access to 'professional expertise' by entering into professional communities. This is a familiar theme in her work. Bolton (1998, p244) says Heathcote has found '... a way of bringing the power of make-believe into the classroom so that her pupils can be 'inside the skin of the expert' and achieve a '... sense of joyous adventure...'

If the stage for this work is online through digital pretexts, serious games or on another platform it does not change the need for students and teachers to be reflective but rather asks us to engage in different ways. When digital drama becomes more commonplace the experience and skills for critical analysis of that work will also grow.

The danger lies in teachers not recognising that they have the skills to support drama learning as they always have, the only difference is it is being played upon another stage. As Haseman says (2004, p23):

> For drama teachers, authenticity is found through a primary commitment to the symbolic capabilities of drama – an aesthetic language with the power to animate the imagination and reframe the future. Then with all the world our stage, the entire content of life is made available for learning, critique and change.

His call for teachers to cling to the essentials of drama and connect with the new world of our students presents a powerful argument for the renewal of our classrooms and approaches to drama learning where the dramatic aesthetic is central and the medium provides the potential for ongoing and seemingly limitless theatrical possibility.

## Conclusion

Just as there is no magic pill to meet our needs for sustenance, there is not, and probably never will be, a drama education classroom without human interaction. There is an implicit contradiction in a drama classroom without real, human players. It may be time to move beyond the fears we harbour and embrace the creative potential we can access when we support human inter-actions with technological tools. Drama educators are living at an exciting and critical time. There has been an explosion in technology that extends and enlivens our art form and provides new and invigorated possibilities for student learning. We have the chance to reject the technology-as-nutrition-pill approach to teaching and find ways to harness its various forms.

The aesthetics of drama are dynamic. The emergence of technologies now and in the future provides further impetus for forms of dramatic expression to ex-pand and change. There will be difficulties in the development of drama and learning working with technology and some of our classroom experiments will fail. We have no choice. Our students are engaging with the technologies around them and importing them into every sphere of their lives, including the theatre they watch and make and the games they play. It is up to drama educators to find appropriate and exciting ways to incorporate the strengths of our pedagogy and the aesthetics of our art form onto these new stages.

If we succeed, we can open up vast new possibilities for creative engagement with the real and virtual worlds our students inhabit and bring the strengths of the drama aesthetic to the online world. Drama educators must avoid creating pointless dichotomies and embrace what is useful in the aesthetics of drama, live and online, for the good of their students.

Chapter 4 explores how theatre companies with young audiences have res-ponded to their digital native audiences. The work examined in Chapter 4 provokes some reassessment of the performance aesthetic which has impor-tant implications for theatrical productions and drama education.

## Notes

**1** New South Wales is the largest state (by population) in Australia. The NSW public schools system is one of the largest school systems in the world.

**2** The NSW Board of Studies develops syllabus and oversees examinations in New South Wales.

**3** Metaxis is '...the state of belonging completely and simultaneously to two different autonomous worlds' (Boal, 1995, p43).

# 4

# Young people and mediated performance

I f they walk into the foyer of Contact Theatre Company in Manchester, instead of the discipline of the formal architecture of traditional theatres, young people encounter a contemporary environment, containing sights and sounds they know. Audiences are involved in the performances, talking and interacting like an Elizabethan audience might have done and in similar ways to audiences at football or a rock concert. The lights are always a little higher than usual so the audience can see each other and be seen. In the performance theatrical light and surround sound mix with projected images, movies, wireless, real time cameras and technology that allows performers to control the performance effects.

Innovative companies such as Contact, and Arena Theatre Company in Melbourne are inviting young audiences to encounter a new form of theatrical experience that is transformed from traditional theatre. This is new theatre for a new audience and it demands innovative and collaborative approaches in the making and performing of the work. As always, one of the central tensions is how technology and the theatrical worlds create theatrical meaning for these audiences. For John E. McGrath, Artistic Director of Contact Theatre Company, using technology is a mandatory feature of developing theatre for his young audiences. He argues that using technology in drama-making is as natural as using other production effects such as lighting. He sees technology as a fully integrated part of his devising process at Contact theatre:

> I am not at all interested in technology as an add-on but I am interested in how technology, how the digital image, how music technology and sound could be left out of the form and the content of the theatre[1].

Young people see technology as integral to their cultural landscape: this is evident in the performances being created for and often by young people. Whilst traditional theatre may be struggling with declining audience numbers and declining revenues, there are exciting innovations emerging in Theatre for Young People which embrace technology and use new forms. This chapter begins with a discussion of some of the ways technology is being integrated into performance: two performance companies who have used theatrical innovation, including technology, to find new audiences for live performance are examined. The work of Contact Theatre in Manchester and Arena in Melbourne provide some insights into how theatre can be reborn and revitalised through understanding how to connect with their audiences.

## Performance and technology

It is simplistic to suggest that technology has always been part of theatre from the *machina* and *skena* of the ancient Greek theatre to the invention of theatrical lighting and more modern descendants such as projected images. At the heart of this discussion is the question of how technology is used to create meaning for young audiences. Before we look at the companies working in these ways, some of the fallacies that relate to working with technology and performance must be challenged.

## Debunking the myths

### Myth 1 Technology and performance should fight each other

In the same way that teachers sometimes see technology and drama education in conflict so too do theatre makers. Auslander (1999, p1) argues that traditionally theatre makers and critics have 'valorised' live over mediatised forms of drama and theatre. He argues that:

> All too often, such analyses take on the air of a melodrama in which virtuous live performance is threatened, encroached upon, dominated, and contaminated by its insidious Other, with which it is locked in a life and death struggle. From this point of view, once live performance succumbs to mediatisation, it loses its ontological integrity. (Auslander, 1999, p1)

Auslander argues that most performances with an audience and performers physically present are mediated in some way, through microphones or sound augmentation for example. They possess 'liveness' but are not unmediated and dividing performance into discrete boxes, live or mediated, in this manner is unhelpful. A more useful approach is to understand and control whatever element you are working with to create an engaging theatrical world for your audience.

*Myth 2 The use of video and other new media is new*

As Noel Jordan (2002) suggests, there is nothing particularly new about new media. He describes projection being used in the work of Vsevold Meyerhold, Erwin Piscator and Czechoslovakian set designer Joseph Svoboda as early as 1925. He argues that like modern theatre makers the multi-media artists of the past were '...responding to the technological advancements of the day and exploring them within the bounds of their theatrical work'. Like John E. McGrath, those who have worked with multi-media technology in the past saw the technology as '...not a means in itself but a further resource available to an artist in their desire to communicate a story, message or theme' (2002, p73).

The companies, artists and practitioners using technology in this way, including those who produce work for a young audience, are only doing what has always been done with new technology: using the resources available to generate dramatic meaning and impetus and aesthetic engagement with audiences. The difference between now and then is that the modern theatre maker has more effective and cheaper technology. We should be less bedazzled and mesmerised at the technology used and concentrate on critical analysis of how all the performance elements, including the new technology, worked or didn't work in the performance.

*Myth 3 We should recreate new technologies (eg games and/or cinema) in the place of live performance because that is what young audiences know and want*

There must be a temptation for theatre makers to reproduce a video game, television programme or a cinematic experience on stage. The logic is simple: 'kids like games/video/movies, we need to engage kids in the theatre, let's make our play stylistically mimic the aesthetics of these forms'. Students beginning in drama do the same thing when improvising, deriving and using the acting techniques and conventions of naturalistic soap-operas. What drama teachers know is that the main challenge is to provide a bridge between what students consume on television and the different aesthetic of the live space. In both cases they miss a fundamental feature of making art that has integrity. Differing art forms require different processes, different approaches and their audiences have different expectations. While Blast Theory's *Uncle Roy All Around You* is influenced by gaming and theatre, it does not fit comfortably into either. There is an attempt to create a new form, not crudely lift one form and slap it in the place of another. John E Mc Grath argues that at the centre of theatre is the unique live experience:

I don't think young people come into theatre wanting to watch cinema or wanting to watch a video AT ALL. I think the worst work we can create imitates those media. They can have it better online. I think we need to find ways of viewing the world that can interact in live stage spaces. The theatrical event is an incredibly valid thing to do with young audiences.

The companies profiled in this chapter are developing theatre that invites all the artistic workers in from the beginning, sometimes with a pretext and sometimes without, to create work from the ground up that will use technology to serve the dramatic meaning, not as a gratuitous add-on. Although this may be seen as chaotic to those used to conventional theatrical approaches, it is attractive for many other artists who like to develop work holistically and collaboratively.

McGrath argues that audiences do react differently to shows with technology as part of the form and content of the production. Audiences' experiences of technology will inform their understanding of live performances including digital and screen-based work. McGrath believes that 'inevitably we are going to bring our relationship to the virtual into a theatre piece'. There is however a qualitatively different experience for audiences in different performances. McGrath says:

> The experience of going to film is very different to the experience of watching television or looking at stuff online. The desiring relationships to the different kinds of image are very different. We do bring all of those relationships when we come to watch theatre and I think they churn all those relationships up in us.

The challenge for an audience is dealing with their preconceptions when faced with new modes of presentation. For young audiences, McGrath says this challenge is not as great. ' I think the exciting thing about working with a younger audience is that there are less expectations of what theatre ought to be and more experience often in working with those other ways of viewing'.

## Theatre (for Young People) for the 21st Century
Michael Anderson remembers seeing a performance at a main stage in Sydney that tried to integrate what was then the exciting new world of the Internet. The play was an import, written by a famous English playwright, and attempted to grapple with technology and live performance. The director decided that if the play was to be about technology he would use technology in its presentation. As usually happens when technology is a production afterthought, the projections and assorted other technical wizardry appeared tacked on at the end rather than integrated effectively with an engaging live experience.

This common theatrical experience illustrates the importance of integrating and understanding the impact of technology. Phillip Auslander suggests that all performance is now 'mediatised' or influenced through our understanding of technology and that 'Whatever distinction we may have had supposed there to be between live and mediatised events is collapsing because live events are becoming more and more identical with mediatised ones' (1999, p32).

In his analysis he looks mainly at the world of Broadway musicals and suggests the development of the spectacular on stage is a reaction to the effects that audiences see on television and film. While this may not apply across all theatre, it is logical that theatre audiences who have grown up with television and cinema will have different expectations as audiences. Whilst there may be an influence, this argument presupposes that audiences in all places desire the same thing. It assumes that audiences who attend film expect the same features of the theatre and on television. Video did not kill theatre. Theatre is as dynamic as ever, so what is it that specifically attracts people to the theatre?

Assumptions about the present generation of theatre audiences may also prove misleading. It is true that they have been raised like the generation before them on new technologies but this does not necessarily mean that computer gaming will kill drama. On the contrary it has spawned and nurtured new forms of dramatic expression like those of the UK's Blast Theory. Theatre and drama are robust forms. Instead of being fatally wounded by emerging technologies, they are integrating them to reach new audiences. Rose Myers, artistic director of Arena argues that young audiences are looking for authentic and unique experiences in the theatre. She argues that young audiences are not homogenous and that they provide unique challenges for theatre makers:

> Our audiences are very demanding. Their boredom factor is high and their bullshit radar is really strong. Many of the audiences that see our shows have never seen theatre before; they have no interest in theatre and fewer expectations. To excite them to the potential of performance is a great creative challenge. The young artists we employ here are responding to the world that they are living themselves. It's not that we are making work for young people because we have to, it's more that we are working with these audiences because that is what's exciting us artistically.

## Blast Theory

Again at the centre of the theatrical interaction is the commitment to the live event, however it is mediated and supported by technology. In what seems to be a call for theatre to welcome mediatisation and to embrace new technologies Blast Theory are looking to renew theatre through using technology as form and content to understand how drama and theatre might reach new audiences. They argue (Blast Theory, 2004) that theatre has changed little since the 18th century but society has changed radically.

> This is not to say that traditional theatre is finished. But in the same way that painting was transformed forever by the arrival of photography it does have to change. Especially if it seeks to reach a new, younger audience and to have cultural impact. (Blast Theory, 2004, p15)

This renewed understanding of how theatre might be transformed has led to exciting non-traditional forms of theatre being created for new audiences.

## Beyond outmoded dichotomies: embracing the brave new worlds

In our mass media and through our community there is much suspicion of the new. Young people's pursuit of the Internet and gaming is generally seen as frivolous or even dangerous – just as television and film once were. There is justification for these suspicions. The Internet offers in one place through blogging a democratic way for your views to be published and sometimes heard. In other places it allows innocent people to be exploited through child pornography. This is the nature of most technology. It can and will be used for building up communities as well as threatening them. Educators have the responsibility to support the criticism and analysis of the content, and to build the skills for young people to be able to experiment and produce things of value, especially art work on this stage. This is the general principle that fires the work of Blast Theory. As artists who emerge from mainstream theatre they see no choice but to engage in theatre that fully embraces and experiments with new and old technologies and in the process create new audiences for a form they call mixed reality.

Figure 4.1: *Uncle Roy All Around You*, 2003. An interactive game played online and on the streets of London using handheld computers.

*Image courtesy of Blast Theory.*

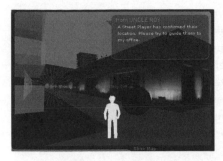

**Figure 4.2: Online players assisted real players by observing their progress and providing assistance**

Their work is a pioneering example of what could be the future of new theatrical forms. They draw from the traditions of the performance art or live-art movement, theatre, film and gaming. They defy categorisation because of their willingness to embrace new ideas and new forms from across the artistic and media spectrums. They describe themselves as artists who ... explore interactivity and the relationship between real and virtual space with a particular focus on the social and political aspects of technology. Their art works with and against the media saturation of western societies '...using video, computers, performance, installation, mobile and online technologies to ask questions about the ideologies present in the information that envelops us' (Blast Theory, 2005).

Blast Theory's most recent work *Uncle Roy All Around You* saw players search for Uncle Roy in an online and a real city. The game used an online player to guide the player in the real street through the city to find Uncle Roy's office. When the players found the office they were asked some questions about trust. If the players indicated that they would trust one of their fellow players they entered into an agreement to 'be contactable' for that person in a time of crisis (for real).

There are several aspects of Blast Theory's work that are innovative, striking and relevant to drama educators. The most obvious is the playing on multiple stages of a game that encourages the taking on of roles as the player or as a feature of the game. Furthermore there is at the centre of the game a pretext that could have been designed by a drama educator. The players are given technology, maps, GPS and mobile phones, to find Uncle Roy's office within a specified time – this is the tension found in any good pretext. When they find him their expectations of what the drama/game is about changes. It is not, as they had expected, about Uncle Roy but rather about our relationships with strangers. Siobhan Murphy from the London Newspaper *Metro* had this experience of the work:

It's gaming made real, a spy film where you're the star. It's exciting some-times hilarious (especially when puzzled policemen feel moved to ask you what exactly you're up to) and other times quite unnerving when you realise someone leaning against a wall has been watching you all along. There's also a message to contemplate...you are asked to make a leap of faith, which may be coloured by your experiences immediately previous to being asked this question. So you leave feeling contemplative, thrilled and ever so slightly paranoid. What more could you ask for in the theatre? (*Metro*, Friday, May 30, 2003, p17)

At the core of Blast Theory's work is not a preoccupation with toys but rather an interest in the use of technology to explore social and artistic questions. Another of their projects *Desert Rain* examines issues related to modern war-fare. It offers a

... disconcerting engagement with understanding of warfare in today's mediatised world. Its shifting exploration of the virtual and the real, of tech-nology and nature, and of mass media and individual experience, are all paralleled in the 'mixed reality' interface technologies. (Wyver, 1999)

The artists in Blast Theory and in other companies like them are attempting to democratise and civilise the technologies they are working with. Their intention is to use technology as a response to the society around them (Blast Theory, 2004) but also as a way of reappraising the arts and transforming whole communities. This is in total contrast to the purveyors of violence and pornography which in the tabloid imagination is associated with these new technologies.

While the demise of traditional theatre has been exaggerated, young people's lack of interest and attendance in the theatre should give us some pause for reflection. Blast Theory's readiness to embrace technology and their artistic and social aims provide teachers with a glimpse of what the future might be in our classrooms and in our theatres. It is up to artists and teachers to take our students into these worlds.

## Technology and performances for young people

Theatre makers and educators who are in Prensky's (2001b) terms digital im-migrants are day by day seeing their classrooms and theatres filled by digital natives with an increasingly sophisticated understanding of technology and new media. In the face of this young audiences are demanding theatre that is relevant to their experiences. Several researchers (Kotler and Scheff, 1997, p224; Kolb, 1997, p142; Brunton, 2004) in the area suggest that young people's attendance is closely linked to their engagement: in other words whether the experience will bore them. This is a challenge for theatre makers who use technology but go beyond it. Like any other audience young people demand a theatrical experience that is relevant and will engage them. This usually includes relevant themes, an engaging narrative and a piece of drama that captures the imagination. There is obviously a role for well-designed, written and implemented technology in this context but the challenge goes beyond technology and demands the invention or evolution of new, more relevant theatrical productions for young people.

Contact Theatre in Manchester and Arena Theatre Company in Melbourne have a tradition of making relevant and dynamic theatre specifically for young audiences. These companies are currently integrating technology into their performance works for a young audience. Both theatre companies and their recent productions are examined and their joint production *Skid 180*, to be performed in Manchester, Melbourne and Sydney in 2006, is discussed.

## Arena Theatre, Melbourne

Melbourne's Arena Theatre Company is an example of a performance group which has engaged young people with creating relevant, dynamic and technologically savvy theatre. Melbourne is the second largest city in Australia with 3.6 million people, of which 8.5 per cent are under the age of 15. Arena's mission is to

> create dynamic contemporary theatre that genuinely engages young audiences. Arena sees young people as at the forefront of new cultural expression, and believes that all young people are entitled to cultural experiences. (Arena, 2005)

Arena began in the 1960s as a Theatre for Young People group working mainly in schools. According to Rose Myers, its mission has always been to create performance that engages young people. The work has changed as the world has changed, even though the core mission has not. Myers describes the way Arena think about their audiences:

> Young people have not had to adapt to computers, they are fluent in the use of computers. This has refined their capacity to be non-linear and to read a diversity of things at once. As an audience they are more image-based and they have a lot more visual literacy because the world has gone that way a lot more. For instance we examine the interdisciplinary form or children's imagination or do work about the formative time of adolescence, which is a very significant time for making connections. We think of our audiences here as being at the fore of new cultural expression and I think that is the artistically exciting aspect of working here[2].

Their performances integrate technology to appeal to their young audiences. In their recent production *Play Dirty* digital technologies formed an integral part of their production. '*Play Dirty* was technically awesome, fusing theatre, rapid image feedback, live and pre-recorded sound and live freestyle moto-cross action' (Arena, 2005).

These performances are an attempt to connect with an audience that is increasingly demanding technology as part of performance. It is also consistent with the manifesto of the company that is to '...contribute to the repositioning of Australian culture as sophisticated and technologically advanced' (Arena, 2005). In drama curricula around the world students are expected to devise their own drama and appreciate the work of other performers. The implication is that young people will be influenced by what they see. More than appreciation, however, young people are expected to be influenced by what they see in their own theatre-making. The pressures of students' interest in technology, the integration of technology in modern performance and school systems mandating studies in ICT are providing significant pressure for changing pedagogical practices. This pressure gives drama educators the opportunity to incorporate all kinds of technologies and allowing students to use them, just as they have used the old technologies such as light and sound, as tools for creation in the drama classroom. As students study such companies and their work they begin to see it as a normal part of the drama aesthetic and will begin to integrate the work into their own devised performances. This will urge teachers and theatre makers to teach and produce work of relevance to these audiences – no small challenge, as it will require a reassessment of the curriculum and expectations in performance.

### Contact Theatre, Manchester: 'what theatre can be'

Contact Theatre is based in Manchester, a city of 2.5 million people. Manchester is a young, diverse city and 41.9 per cent are aged 24 and under. Contact Theatre, which is situated in a purpose-built facility in Manchester city, is one of the major performing arts venues. It employs 20 to 30 full-time and project-based staff. In the financial year 2003-2004 Contact delivered 84 programmes, productions and events. These were a mix of touring events, events produced by Contact and other programmes such as emerging artists' workshops. Contact is a vibrant, active and large theatre company devoted solely to young audiences.

Contact's aim is to explore what theatre can be for the next generation. Their focus is on 13-30 year-olds as participants, as artists and audiences. The artists and participants are across the age spectrum but the focus of the work is on people age 13 to 30. Contact describe themselves in their annual report as 'a space that welcomes artists, participants, audiences and visitors from many backgrounds' (Contact Theatre, 2004, p5). Contact has been conceived and appears really to be a crucible of ideas and forms. At its centre is the philosophy of participation in all areas of their work. They describe the mix:

> In our participatory emerging and professional work we mix, drama, dance, multimedia spoken word, comedy, slams, club nights, events, exhibitions, showcases, poetry, physical theatre, hip-hop, film, live art and debates to explore what theatre can be. (Contact Theatre, 2004, p5)

Even a casual visitor to Contact Theatre can sense the uniqueness of what this company is attempting and seems to be achieving. Beyond adapting traditional theatre and repackaging it for younger audiences, they start with the central question: what is the potential of theatre for young people and how can we change it, using young people's interests to engage our audiences? The answer is to allow young people to be active participants as well as audiences. John E. McGrath explains the uniqueness of this approach: 'So it's not the traditional TYP model of professional company produces shows as audiences and then runs work around that. Contact engages young people at every level'.

John E. McGrath is a celebrated theatre director and author. His work focuses in part on the uses of surveillance in art and theatre. His interest in technology, media and popular culture have supported him in developing a new vision of what theatre might be in the lives of young people. He initially trained in theatre in New York, working in interdisciplinary companies that used technology in the development of their work. He says of his approach to the job at Contact that it fulfilled a vision to

> ... put young people and artists at the heart of its activity. So my goal was to throw away any traditional models of how a repertory theatre might behave, and to rebuild it as a creative community from the ground up, allowing the artists to interact with the audiences, and creating an atmosphere that was challenging, exciting, and constantly changing.[3]

He sees technology as an integrated part of his theatrical practice. And he sees the central question as not just about form but as relating to the subject matter of everyday life – the role of the virtual and the digital. *Skid 180* is a co-production between Arena and Contact that strives for engagement with their young audiences through examining technology in form and content.

## *Skid 180*: radical performance process

**Figure 4.3: publicity images for *Skid 180***

In 2006 and 2007 Arena and Contact will present *Skid 180* to audiences in Manchester, Sydney and Melbourne. *Skid's* development is a useful example of how theatre is being made by these companies. The production is a global collaboration that uses technology and young artists to tell a story familiar to young audiences. The story is about McStone, a young man in Manchester's BMX sub-culture.

> ...after leaving one world of his nightmares, wakes in another. In his previous world he was in isolation, in this new one he encounters a new 4Real family in the underpass. The 4Real mode of transport is revolutionary wheels, and in their job as couriers, they have a unique view of the city... When the city tries to get one over them, they bite back with style. http://www.arenatheatre. com.au/livework/skid180_synopsis.html .

### The beginning of *Skid*

The project began as an arranged marriage between Contact and Arena. Others spotted the natural synergy between the approaches of the two companies. While global collaboration of this complexity has not always been

70

easy, it has begun an exciting cross-cultural dialogue between artists in Manchester and Melbourne. Tamsin Drury[4] was one of the artistic collaborators at the beginning of *Skid's* devising process.

> It hatched as a small project where Arena, Digital Summer, Contact and a group of young people came together to do a showing with as a work in progress on the mainstage. It was pretty high tech. Miraculously it was pretty good although the development of it was pretty hellish. So we had some main performers, some lads who John found hanging out in the foyer and a gang of BMX riders.

The early development of Skid recalled by Tamsin Drury highlights some significant features of the creative processes that typify these companies. Young people who had an interest in the BMX scene in Manchester were brought into the creative process. Though this may not have been a traditional approach to the making of work, having the potential audience present during the development of the work adds a palpable authenticity to its development. Rather than just mouthing the rhetoric of youth engagement in the arts, in *Skid* Contact and Arena have made it integral to the development of the work.

## Evolving the production

In contrast to the development of a traditional scripted work, Skid brought audience, visual artists and writers into the evolutionary development process from the beginning. This allows the theatre-makers to make discoveries, sometimes serendipitously, about the work. Actors and directors have made such discoveries for centuries but in this emergent form the artists are making discoveries beyond acting. John E. McGrath explains the writers role in this process:

> *Skid* has been workshopped from the earliest days so ideas about the digital and the visual have been informing the script right from early on. Rose has felt that she should and could with the visual artists, have a very strong input into where the story should go. Recently Rose had a workshop with the digital artists and Rose sent Louise (the writer) some quite 'directed' and quite strong ideas. 'We would like the script to do this at this point, why don't you change this and make this happen'. Traditionally a writer in theatre would be pretty resistant but a) Louise was up for that and b) I was able to be the person in Manchester who could support her through that process. I have to say the outcome of that input has been incredibly positive. That piece of input has got the script after many years of development to the point where it feels like a finished product.

The creative team on *Skid 180* are making discoveries about how all the elements including writing, lighting and sound projection work together with the acting to create the show. Rose Myers explains one of the discoveries made by the team about the nature of video as part of the development of *Skid* that puts people into a relaxed state. She says:

> It feels quite dreamlike and the way you consume it is quite different. I think that is what came out of the development, we didn't start out thinking 'video' but rather we threw a whole lot of things together and then thought this is really useful here and let's try and take that quality and push it more.

This process demands enormous time, patience and flexibility for everyone involved. Quite apart from the difficulties that technology brings to the process, the collaborative nature of the development process means that there are several voices demanding attention. A performance that integrates technology effectively may demand this kind of effort. This way of making theatre responds to the changing audience and tools at the disposal of the theatre makers. Such renewed dynamism is a good sign for the ongoing health of theatre for young people.

## Conclusion

There is something significant happening in theatre at the moment. Rather than settling for the status quo and doing what they have always done, there are several companies attempting to change theatre. This change is vital as it has the potential to revitalise the way theatre evolves, not just for young audiences but for all audiences. It is not possible or useful to unravel technology or media from the creative mix that is a feature of this emergent theatre. What we can say is that technology is there in the form and content of the work. It is not a gimmicky add-on but a central element used in the collaborative development of performances.

## Notes

1 This quote is from an interview with John E. McGrath from 22 September 2005. All quotes from him refer to this interview unless otherwise stated.

2 This quote is from an interview with Rose Myers from 24 October 2005. All quotes from her refer to this interview unless otherwise stated.

3 These quotes come from a profile of McGrath on the National Endowment for Science, Technology and the Arts. http://www.nesta.org.uk/ourawardees/profiles/5021/index.html

4 This quote is from an interview with Tamsin Drury from 9 September 2005. All quotes from her refer to this interview.

# 5

## Theatre in Education:
## devising dramatic property

The scene is a small market town in rural Hertfordshire England, on an early spring morning. A white van rolls into the car park at the local high school. The students, jostling and chatting while getting ready for their drama class, take no notice of it. The roof of the van slides quietly back and a hydraulic lift powers a complex shape that fans out into large satellite dish that tracks across the morning sky to lock onto a communication satellite far above the atmosphere. An uplink connection is made and suddenly the school has wireless Internet coverage. Two young people get out of the van and unload a suite of wireless laptops equipped with high-speed broadband access. C&T, the visiting Theatre in Education team has arrived and the drama class is ready to begin!

In this chapter we focus on C&T, a Theatre in Education Company and their use of technology and drama in a wide range of educational settings.

Paul Sutton, Director and teacher with C&T explains:

> ...our drama programmes, although they use technology, are designed to inspire individuals from every background to learn about the world around them and widen participation in the performing arts'[1].

C&T's self sufficient approach to technology and information access allows them to travel to wherever they are needed, so the learning spaces occupied by the students can be as flexible as the drama programmes they deliver. From inner city schools to rural communities they link technology and drama together in new and exciting ways for young people.

## Some background on Theatre in Education

Theatre in Education traces its origins from the late 1960s in Australia and the United Kingdom (O'Toole and Bundy, 1993, p134) and from the early 1970s in the United States (Swortzell, 1993). While the TIE movements differed according to their contexts, they all shared the same aim: '...to provide an experience for children that will be intensely absorbing, challenging, even provocative, and an unrivaled stimulus for further work chosen in the subject in and out of school' (Jackson, 1993, p1).

Michael Anderson recalls the TIE companies visiting his primary school in Australia in the late 1970s:

> I saw what seemed like an enormous amount of TIE as a primary school child in Western Sydney. My primary school was in one of the poorest parts of Sydney. It received government funding and companies were subsidised to bring their shows. Typically the visit would occur on a day that happened to be the hottest of the year and most of the school (about 1200 children) were crammed into the most inappropriate space for public performance, the school hall. While the token ceiling fans whirred noisily overhead a group of often very skilled actors performed a show about the dangers of well, whatever was dangerous at the time. You name it: drugs, alcohol, pushbikes, etc. My memory of these performances ranges from some of the most wonderful performances I have seen, to the banal and didactic.

> Some productions bore out Alex Buzo's claim that '...the TIE people do a great job educating children, but it's not art and it's not entertainment' (Buzo, 1988 cited in O'Toole and Bundy, p137). Others soared and inspired with stunning theatricality. These performances were made all the more astonishing given the circumstances these companies had to perform in and the pittance they must have been paid. It is my guess that most kids had their first (and for many) their only experience of the theatre in this way. After the performers had finished they left in their clapped out old bus or van. Occasionally there would be an 'education pack' to extend the performance for students, but anything beyond that was a rarity.

In the UK, where the funding was more realistic, TIE took the form of a programme of work rather than a one-off performance. It was:

> ...a structured pattern of activities, usually devised and researched by the company, around a topic of relevance both to the school curriculum and the students own lives, presented in the school by the company and involving the children directly in an experience of the situations and problems that the situation throws up'. (Jackson, 1993, p4)

This was a far cry from the mass performance models familiar in Australian TIE. Gavin Bolton believes that TIE at its best can create an authentic theatrical experience for children.

> The actors can create three dimensionality and with immediacy, a believable context that arrests attention and interest and above all, creates the potential for a multi-level experience of theatre…The context itself can be rich in meaning and significant for the children, not simply as a vivid simulation but also because it taps into universal and personal connotations of meaning that all theatre provides. (Bolton, 1993, p47)

The company C&T started its life with a traditional Theatre in Education approach but now engages students in a new drama aesthetic, combining theatre with digital technology. It is producing exciting online role devised scenarios based on interactive audience participation within live and mediated performance. These online scenarios provide students with a series of pretexts and framed interactions that introduce and deepen the drama. As Paul Virilio (1989, p66) points out, in the current digital world of computers, gaming, video and cellphones, we are all, and especially young people, becoming 'directors of our own reality', and these alternative forms of performance based information are used as resources along with the wider informational resources of the digital world.

Although the theoretical framework adopted by C&T grew out of the UK approach to Theatre and Drama in Education, their work is based on the developing multimodal communication environment many young people already operate daily. New communication patterns and rapid changes in learning styles shifted many students in their everyday life from 'reading the world' as have expressed in written texts to reading the world as portrayed in image, sound and text (Kress, 2003). C&T see students as accessing this world with a wireless laptop computer or whatever digital delivery system is available as a way of opening the vast range of information available online for access and interaction. For C&T the certainty of given knowledge in the older print-based world becomes more contingent when part of such an open-ended interactive media environment. The company links interaction in the dramatically devised forms of Theatre in Education and blends it with a range of technoliteracy skills to provide powerful new learning insights for the participants.

## Technoliteracy and drama

Technoliteracy (Lankshear, Snyder and Green, 2000) is the term used when meaning making is linked to new and emerging forms of technology. The multi-platform digital interactions of games and computers that constitute young people's everyday communication and entertainment framework also account for much of their current knowledge, interests and skill base. The modes of representation they favour in their everyday lives are central to incorporating drama and technology as a form of pedagogy and as social practice in the emerging popular cultural aesthetic.

Young people, at least in the West, live in a culture full of mediated dramatic narrative, television, film, and increasingly immersive video gaming. It is a culture where more people shape their understanding of the world through mediated forms of drama like television soap operas and video games than ever before. The visual and textual forms captured and projected into most homes are shaping the performance preferences of everyone. The effect of new technology is most obvious in the young. The shift to a digital native environment needs to be studied and used for educational purposes as well as for entertainment and communication. Companies such as C&T are doing this as they use the technoliteracy of their young participants for drama and cultural education.

### Case study: C&T

Established in 1988 and now based at the University of Worcester, C&T began working in the UK model of TIE practice. But an increasing focus on technology in applied theatre settings did not sit comfortably with traditional TIE practices. By using role-based workshop approaches and process drama, the company continued to work in schools and community settings, using the dramatic forms pioneered by Dorothy Heathcote, applying her techniques to media and technology related topics. Their research perspective is focused on the relationship between drama, young people and technology, producing interesting and innovative hybrid performance forms. The company focuses on the meanings and influence being generated by the evolving digital culture and its impact on the lives of their target audiences. Influenced theoretically by Raymond Williams' (1990) descriptions of the dramatized society and the impact of television on culture, they have extrapolated this approach into online cultural forms.

The projects described in this case study illustrate how one TIE company is responding to ways in which new technologies reconstruct notions of reality and liveness (Auslander, 1999) in performance. The company's use of performers in multiple roles, both embodied and virtual, is designed to offer a reflexive critique of current mainstream media forms and the power and influence they wield in society at large. C&T examine these issues of media representation though a range of multimodal texts respond to the contemporary interests and concerns of young people.

Rather than theorising the evolving relationship between media, education and drama, their programmes incorporate everyday digital technologies, allowing them to tap into the energy of young people's involvement in digital popular culture. One of their most innovative concepts in the application of a technological approach to the outcomes of drama is their idea of a 'dramatic property'.

## The dramatic property

By becoming reflexively media orientated and pioneering the use of multimedia technology platforms and cultural practices, C&T have evolved a unique model of what they have called a 'dramatic property' (Sutton, 2005) (see Chapter 1). Content is trancodifed from one dramatic form to another. It is based on the different modes of representation afforded by digital technology and the ability of young people to use the skills of technoliteracy to become co-creators of content (Cope and Kalanzis, 2000).

Different delivery platforms account for many of the varieties of interaction occurring in young people's lives, such as digital games, computers and mobile phones, along with more overtly text-based linguistic modes such as texting, instant messaging and chat rooms. By deliberately integrating the drama content across this range of platforms the company has utilised a developing youth culture aesthetic of transcodified multimodal material, facilitated through a common range of technoliteracy skills. Paul Sutton explains:

> What C&T did was to ask the question, 'well if we take this idea of living in a dramatised technological society, how do we proceed, in terms of the diverse ways that young people use all those kinds of media cultures to engage them in drama?'

The company saw how the converging digital technologies and the convergence of media forms meant that young people were not only the consumers of the dramatised society around them but were increasingly the producers of it too. The introduction of the active producer element into their dramatic work signaled a shift in the power balance between audience and performer. It opened up the possibility for theatre to have a different relationship with its audience, instead of sitting in rows and listening. The audience become active participants in the process of production. C&T saw their audience as digital natives in the same way as Prensky, (2001b) portrays them: as digital natives with interactive media skills, able to make the technology work for them to influence dramatic outcomes. Young people were seen as more literate and capable than the school curriculum acknowledges. They were treated not just as audience but as participants and co-designers of the drama process. They could use their technoliteracy skills to access and shape the material being presented, and could move easily from one form of mediated content to another. As active producers, young people are constantly transferring (or transcoding) their understanding of one medium into another. This is seen whenever they apply their understanding of process drama conventions to video production (Mooney, 2004) or when file sharing and manipulating music and vision from computer and DVD sources.

### The Dark Theatre

One of the C&T's most successful early projects at this trancodification of content into an alternative dramatic text was *The Dark Theatre*, in which schools use drama to create a range of student-devised comic books. The structure of *The Dark Theatre* was a murder/mystery/who-done-it in comic book form. Each term one issue of the comic would be published for parti-cipating schools. Embedded in the narrative of the comic were activities and tasks, predominantly of role-play performances and process drama based activities which the students would have to engage with, perform and ulti-mately transform. The results of this dramatic work were fed back to the com-pany and in turn informed the writing of the next issues of the comic. So although it was a murder mystery, the company didn't know the outcome when they began. The students authored the text with the company as part of the creative process. The company was keen to work in this collaborative way and was aware early on of the synergies, of vertical integration and how those processes could work across different media forms. They started from a low-tech base – comic books – but what was particularly interesting was the way they were trying to develop collaborative authorship of the content. As Paul Sutton, the Director of the company puts it:

> We were trying to use those principles behind the work of Roland Barthes, the idea of interrogating text, having text where the reader has an active en-gagement with it and authors it. The student's work became incredibly cryptic and very dense in terms of the way that it tried to operate. This density of content is quite often created in the imaginations of the students within a drama. The students applied a narrative fiction to the comics and built layer upon layer of content, which might not have been there when it was originally written. This encouraged the notion; you are only going to get to the bottom of the mystery if you interrogate it. This became part of the narrative structure of the drama.

**Figure 5.1: C&T's *Dark Theatre* comic, issue 2**

The new balance of content and form that grew out of *The Dark Theatre*, along with the idea of vertical integration, seemed to the company to have a synergy with the way traditional TIE worked: as a stimulus or pretext for drama. In traditional TIE, performers often use a text or small objects to engage the audience/participants in different dramatic starting points. This use of a pretext seemed to the company to be a way for participants in a TIE programme to leap between one mediated version of the text to another and provide cross-fertilization of ideas within a drama process. This idea of the vertical integration of drama material played strongly to a way of working with theatre in education across different mediums. The company began to work with e-mail, digital video, a Web page or a message service as a pretext for drama.

What the company saw, in a way similar to process drama, was how the kinds of layering of different stimuli in *The Dark Theatre* deepens the sense of meaning in the drama. It saw echoes of this process in popular culture. In consumer terms, a young person might go and see a film and then buy the sound track to the film, and the video game of the same material. The content of the original form encouraged young people to buy in and associate with the film franchise or commercial artistic artifacts. In a similar way, there seemed to be potential for multiple drama forms in digital media, and across the cultural industries more broadly. When C&T examined comic book industry business models and practices they found that Marvel Comics had transformed themselves from being solely a comic book publisher to a company based on the characters of their publications. Marvel talked about these character-based properties such as Spiderman or Captain America as their core business and rebranded the company as Marvel Characters.

These character based properties are deployed across a whole range of different media forms on television, cartoon and films, t-shirts as well as comics. C&T decided that since TIE and process drama had the same kind of open-ended structure, it might be possible to apply the same principles to it. The comic characters have a mythological quality – the narratives about the superheroes that embark on endless adventures can be reinvented or reinterpreted for new generations. Improvised drama has the same open structure, so young people could be part of constructing the dramatic roles and media delivery system. The use of character based digital drama encompassed the idea of a dramatic property and allowed for the consolidation of intellectual property and the transcodification and reuse of it. Paul Sutton explains:

> This concept of the digital 'dramatic property' developed by C&T for *The Dark Theatre* was already part of mainstream media thinking but had not

been applied in a systematic way to student work developed from an educational drama base.

C&T approached process dramas and TIE as dramatic properties in the same way. The company saw these cultural artifacts as products of collaborative work, a shaped form of intellectual property that could be deployed across different kinds of dramatising media. What they saw as important was the ability that process drama and theatre in education both have: the use of different dramatic conventions to reinforce a central learning objective. It seemed possible to take a dramatic property and transform it in the same way by using different media formats to express its meaning. Participants would then have several experiences that emerged from the original dramatic property, including and extending beyond the TIE experience.

C&T's approach has a plasticity and fluidity about it because of its connection and focus on digital media, which allows the dramatic property to take on an extended life. The drama is no longer restricted to the ephemeral moment of performance. The intellectual property underpinning the work could be transcoded and adapted to work across different media. The company's aim is to make the dramatic property work just as well online as it does on stage or DVD or a computer game. The dramatic experience for the participants will be different in terms of the media platform and delivery but will share the same high quality aesthetic experience. It responds to the desire of young people to become part of the production process in any dramatic construct. Passive spectatorship and the discipline of the cultural and physical space of the traditional theatre is not an option for the young people working with C&T. They expect to participate in any artistic experience.

As Paul Sutton says:

> Young people want to participate. They want to take part. Here's an example. When the UK Arts Council was doing the theatre review...they asked us to run a workshop with young people. We did it as a consultation exercise so that the Arts Council senior managers could see what young people were interested in. We did a short drama exercise of what they wanted to get out of theatre and there were about 30 or 40 young people there. Ninety five per cent of them wanted to participate in drama. They didn't see themselves as audiences. The Arts Council officials were tearing their hair out saying 'But where is the audience? Some of you have to go to the theatre because we have all these theatres with seats and you have just got to go. You can't all be on stage. If people ever only want to be on stage theatre is doomed'. The officials didn't get it. Young people want to be part of the process. They didn't want to be passive.

The producer/consumer ethic he identifies is how C&T works. By encouraging a different kind of participatory practice with their audiences and running workshops that reflect young people's own priorities rather than submitting to the requirements of the theatre establishment, C&T taps into the energy of the cultural integration of transcodified cultural product across the media. This is where the artistic and cultural energy exists in society today and the young people respond enthusiastically. As Paul Sutton again explains:

> If young people's dramatic vocabulary is so profoundly informed by the media texts of our dramatised society, then why should not theatre, the dramatic form from which all others derive, not appropriate the conventions, techniques and technologies of these media to construct new and original theatre texts designed to engage these media literate audiences?' (Shaughnessy, 2003)

## The Livingnewspaper.com

The outcome was their ambitious DVD and Web based dramatic property, The Living Newspaper. It examines how the media operate in western culture.

C&T describes their thelivingnewspaper.com Website as:

> a global network of ordinary people – young people – making their voice heard, exploring ideas, challenging expectations, playing their part in the drama of world events. Using an innovative mix of drama and ICT the living newspaper.com is a unique network, researching, exploring and dramatising major international news stories as they break. The livingnewspaper.com gives a unique insight into the things that matter to young people – enabling them to articulate their thoughts, feelings and ideas about world events as they happen.

The dramatic frame is supported by a complex and multilayered CD-ROM that provides the pretext and content for dramatic exploration by participants. Within this dramatic frame a covert network of young people is encouraged to sign up to challenge the media's expectations of what young people are interested and concerned with. The CD-ROM is an online distance-learning tool, based partly on the idea of a documentary drama form of theatre from the 1930s. Like this earlier documentary drama form, The Living Newspaper aims wider than dramatic fiction. It is designed to deconstruct the media messages that are part of everyday culture and provide a place for resistance and critique.

Nicola Shaughnessy (2005, p206) describes how it functions:

> ... participants (generally school pupils) operate in a controlling authoring role; they decide on an issue they want to explore (examples have included the use of CCTV, school closures and asylum seekers) and use the resources supplied by C&T ...Teachers and young people work alongside the company, learning a range of techniques for documentation and production.

As Shaughnessy (2005) points out, it even includes a manifesto to highlight the themes of media constructedness and young people's participation, understanding and criticism of it. It proclaims:

---

### Manifesto Livingnewspaper.com

- The Living Newspaper does not exist.

- The idea of a covert organization committed to uncovering the truth behind the drama of world events is ridiculous.

- To believe that the world's news media at best ignore young people, at worst twist and distort what they say, do, think and feel, is self delusion.

- And that this network, through its strength in creativity, might actually change the world for the better is the biggest joke of all.

- The idea is pure theatre.

- Face facts.

---

As participants take up the challenge of the manifesto and interact with the drama they

> ...are invited to 'sign-up' to a covert network called *thelivingnewspaper.com*. This covert network comprises of a number of 'Cells' of documentary drama activists once inducted, these Cells (effectively a school...) are charged with researching, investigating and dramatising topical news stories...The Command and Control functions of the covert network are led by a small, anonymous and highly secretive team, who issue instructions and advice to participants through the Website (Sutton and Shaughnessy, 2002).

The drama proceeds through a complex self-aware process; the students know they are involved in a dramatic frame similar to videogaming and have online personas but the content has a reality and urgency rarely present in school activities. This edginess is part of the appeal and is acknowledged by the company. Paul Sutton again:

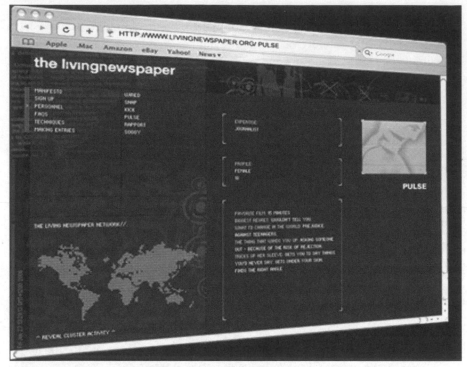

**Figure 5.2: Screenshot of C&T's *Living Newspaper***

What drove C&T into using digital technologies, as part of what we did was the fact that this was implicit in the way young people use those technologies. I think all the notions that worry teachers and those people who kind of supervise, monitor young people and protect young people is in this use. The fact that you can change your identity, have a different e-mail address, all those things that are what young people like. Hiding themselves or reinventing themselves on-line is what they engage in. I think this was a starting point for a lot of the work. The capacity to lose themselves in those kinds of worlds was what was fun and engaging about it.

Beyond using the technology, C&T are also examining the perennial preoccupation of adolescence: the search for and experimentation with identity. The role distance available to participants through identification with online characters allows young people scope for discovery and experimentation without the penalties they might incur in other forums.

## Conclusion

In 1993 Lowell Swortzell wrote a critical chapter on the state of TIE.

> When are we going to explore what TIE might gain from the techniques of circus, vaudeville, mime, puppetry, mixed media, musical comedy, clowning, improvisation, the living newspaper and so on ... I am here to plead that we put theatre back into TIE – before it dies in the desert. And it has already run out of water and is crawling on its knees. (Swortzell, 1993, p248-249)

While this may be somewhat exaggerated – TIE is strong in many places – the call for dynamism and change is justified. C&T seem to have embraced Swortzell's vision for a change in the form and style of TIE to avert 'dying in the desert'. The companies described in this book are involved in a struggle to become relevant for their audiences of increasingly media savvy young people.

C&T's approach provides a way forward for TIE, perhaps out of Swotzell's metaphorical desert. *The Dark Theatre* demonstrates the company's understanding of how dramatic property can be used to move a process drama into another medium. In the *livingnewspaper.com* they have created a role based, online drama that challenges students through a game-based approach to develop an awareness of how the media works. The significance of their work for drama educators is in the way they transform pretext driven drama into an online role-based form. Their work indicates what might be possible if educators gain access to the resources and ideas to support the development of drama and the powerful intellectual concept of role-based dramatic properties. In Chapter 6 we examine other approaches that might be developed in the drama classroom and applied theatre contexts through two further case studies, *To The Spice Islands* and *Flood*.

## Notes
1 This quote is from an interview with Paul Sutton, Director of C&T on 27 June 2005. All quotes from him are from this interview unless otherwise stated.

# 6

## Drama, education and technology:
## case studies of situated role

I magine a classroom unbounded by the limits of the knowledge of the teachers and students within it. Imagine a space where the collective knowledge of humankind could be accessed to enrich learning. Imagine in this space a group of young people busily engaged in a complex professional task, engaged with their bodies and their minds, describing in the language of the profession, whether they are engineers, journalists, or marine archaeologists, how they would fulfil a commission they have been set or solve a pressing social problem.

This chapter outlines how this imaginary classroom already exists and how everyday, even routine technology is combined with well-known process drama approaches – specifically pretexts – to create authentic dramatic contexts for students of all ages. The implication for teachers is that currently existing and now quite commonplace technologies can form the basis of dynamic dramatic experiences without the need to find (or fund) vast new technological resources.

The realities of drama students' everyday lives is the raw material of drama education (see Chapter 1). Without them teachers struggle to anchor the drama in ways that will be relevant and engaging for students. We are not precluding studies of theatre or playscripts which have their own educational rationale, but arguing that drama experiences are best grounded in the everyday lives of our students.

This chapter describes two learning and teaching projects that use readily available digital media and Internet technology, combined with a pretext of a professional commission, to create powerful mediated learning communities.

The first case study is a drama research project designed around student learning experiences that combine process drama and role-based digital interactivity. The *To the Spice Islands* case study describes how the dramatic conventions of process drama, when combined with the immersive qualities of everyday digital networks, can generate a hybrid form of dramatic engagement and performance we have called *situated role*. It uses the now common-place digital technologies of the Internet, e-mail, Weblogs and video recording to develop a digital pretext for process drama.

The second case study, *Flood*, is an applied theatre project that uses more advanced computer-based simulation using artificial intelligence (AI) software known as *chatterbots* to aid students using role performance. This applied theatre project was developed around a training simulation for tertiary journalism students, and used a free Web-based service to create a virtual character whom students could interview. This case study illustrates how even relatively low level simulations can use freely available technology to engage students and establish a dramatic frame to enable learning.

## Case Study 1: The *To the Spice Islands* project
## Combining process drama and role-based digital interactivity

> Excuse me. Do you know where there are any personages of historical signi-
> ficance around here? *Bill and Ted's Excellent Adventure* (1989)

In the film *Bill and Ted's Excellent Adventure,* two time-travelling teenagers on the verge of failing their history assignment 'most heinously' decide to collect famous figures for their class presentation. During this comical adventure new contemporary narratives are built around historical figures such as Abraham Lincoln, Joan of Arc and Socrates.

This case study describes a school-based project that allowed interaction with people and events from more than three centuries ago. *To the Spice Islands* was a computer-mediated learning experience that brought together Dutch tertiary drama students and primary school children to generate a collective dramatic narrative about the shipwreck of a Dutch merchant ship, *Batavia*, off the Western Australian coast in 1629. While Bill and Ted had access to a time-travelling telephone booth to complete their history class, this project combined role-based drama and online historical research to actively engage the participants in contextual learning of curriculum content and enrol them in a community of practice as marine archaeologists.

## What is a digital pretext?

Pretext is the occasion that initiates dramatic action, providing a firm base for the dramatic encounter; such that:

> ...the function of the pre-text is to activate the weaving of the text of the process drama. As well as indicating that it not only exists prior to the text but also relates to it'. (O'Neill, 1995, p20)

By extending the concept of pretext in process drama, this project attempted to use the world of digital technology as a context for drama. As O'Neill and others see it, the pretext operates as a 'holding form' (Witkin, 1974) for the meanings inherent in the dramatic content and helps to establish the location, roles and situation of the drama. Pretext helps to frame the participants in a clear relationship with the potential action of the drama and defines the nature and extent of the dramatic world. In turn, it implicitly defines the range of roles available to the participants in the drama and generates expectations about the first moment of interaction that will start the drama.

This concept of pretext was applied as a guiding principle for the *To the Spice Islands* project, which as well as establishing an online environment, adopted the following process drama features outlined by Philip Taylor (1995) as part of its overall design:

- separate scenic units linked in an organic manner
- thematic exploration
- an experience that does not depend upon a written script
- a concern with participants' change in outlook
- improvisational activity
- outcomes not predetermined but discovered in process
- a script generated through action
- the project leader actively working within and outside the drama.

The extension of the concept of pretext combined with process drama conventions in the digital domain was based on matching levels of dramatic engagement with increasing levels of digital interactivity. In this way it was hoped that the digital pretext of the drama would evolve organically, allowing for a growing internal logic and coherence with the qualities of a good pretext and good drama. Cecily O'Neill (1995, p136) defines the qualities of a good pretext for process drama as:

- responsiveness to imaginative transformation
- the tensions, changes or contrasts it suggests

■ the questions it raises about identity and society, power and possibility

■ the power to launch the dramatic world with economy and clarity, propose action and imply transformation.

While the dramatic conventions of historically framed process drama are well understood within the drama field (Neelands and Goode, 2000), the pervasiveness of digital technologies within school classrooms means that the use of a computer constructed pretext may provide new avenues for the development of dramatic role performance conventions. This case study of a digital pretext-based research project illustrates one such approach.

## Designing the *To the Spice Islands* project

The project was specifically designed as an experiment in digital multi-platform dramatic learning using a digital pretext. It used the power of small-scale social connectivity and the narrative interactivity inherent in the process drama form to play to the strengths of the digital interface with young people. The methodology was designed to increase levels of interactivity as levels of dramatic involvement in the project increased. Thus the project developed from a simple text-heavy Website to include e-mail, Weblog entries, digital video clips and ultimately digital and live performance.

The participants were two classes of Dutch upper primary pupils (age 10-12) and a group of Dutch tertiary drama students. The project coordinators were two Australian teachers with backgrounds in drama and Web production.

The online element of the drama project was built around the pretext of a Website for a fictional organisation, the Australian/Netherlands Maritime Research Centre (ANMRC). Construction started with a simple Web page template incorporating a mock logo and internal navigation links. The material was deliberately modelled as if it were a real site, both aesthetically and technologically; there was no difference between the look and function of the drama-based site and any non-drama site. The site is hosted on Charles Sturt University's public Web server and can be accessed on the Web at http://www.csu.edu.au/newmedia/batavia/ .

The dramatic frame and conventions of the drama were established when two tertiary drama students made a first brief visit to the school classroom. Performing in dramatic role as ANMRC representatives, they introduced the topic and the tension necessary for dramatic engagement in the project, which in this case was a request for help to solve the mystery behind a recently discovered letter from the 17th Century. It was made clear to the pupils

**Figure 6.1: Digital video still of letter being read on board the *Batavia***

that this was a drama project and that although the letter was a dramatic construct it was based on similar historically accurate documents.

The letter concerned the fate of a child on board a Dutch East India ship, the *Batavia*. The students were told this historical document had been found in an archive in Australia. The drama students, still in role as marine archaeologists, enlisted the aid of the pupils as researchers on the Website, in their quest to uncover the mystery surrounding the letter. This engaged the students with the basic digital pretext behind the project and co-opted their assistance to develop the narrative, which Ryan (1997) argues is important to the success of an interactively generated dramatic work.

The Website originally consisted of a template of sub-sections based on topics or research areas related to the project such as marine archaeology, the

Dutch spice trade, and Dutch shipwrecks on the Australian coast. A simple Web page was created for each of these topics and some links to genuine existing online resources were added to provide initial content. An e-mail account was opened at the free Web-based service, Hotmail, to provide an initial point of contact between the drama students in role as ANMRC archaeologists and the school students in their new drama role as trainee marine archaeologists. The e-mail also added to the functionality of the fictional site, increasing its credibility as a pretext in the developing dramatic narrative. The pupils were encouraged to post their thoughts and research on the possible background and meaning of the recently discovered letter.

Further original project content was added to Website topic pages as the Dutch drama students and the school pupils began to provide their own research material. The first visual contribution to the site by the school children was in the form of a digital photo gallery. Portrait shots of each student were taken with a digital camera and the Web gallery was generated automatically using Adobe Photoshop software. These shots were added to the project site with a link to 'meet our latest assistants', and the pupils were labelled ANMRC trainees, thus helping to further establish their commissioned role in the project/performance.

As levels of dramatic engagement and commitment built up, short digital movies were being shot in the Netherlands and transferred to the Website as Apple QuickTime video files. The first batch featured the drama students introducing themselves in role as ANMRC trainee marine archaeologists and highlighting their specialisations. These were added to the Website in both QuickTime and Windows Media format using Media Cleaner Pro software. The children were encouraged to contact the ANMRC staff first by e-mail and later by the online journal tool commonly known as a Weblog. While the Website was taking shape, a Weblog was created using the free service provided by blogger (www.blogger.com) to enable this dialogue to happen. The Dutch drama students, while operating in role as marine archaeologists, used this form of interactivity to communicate personally with the pupils/trainees. The Weblog was dramatically framed in the present as a diary created by the trainee archaeologists that built up a lively record of speculation and research ideas between the school pupil trainees and the drama student experts.

When the dramatic conventions and techniques of using the Weblog between the ANMRC and the trainee marine archaeologists had been firmly established a further dramatic convention of the *Timescope* was introduced. This dramatic device, instantly understood and appropriated by the children as a way to see into the past, through a time telescope, started to produce historical moments in QuickTime video format. The pupils had established by researching the Web that the ship was the *Batavia* and became deeply involved in the historical research of the pretext and emotionally involved in the plight of a child on board the ship.

A second Weblog allowed passengers and crew on board the *Batavia* to communicate with the school pupils via the conventions of the fictional *Timescope* technology. The tertiary drama students were provided with the passwords and access privileges that would allow them to create and edit the Weblogs themselves, using the Web-based interface provided by blogger.

A link to the *Timescope* Weblog was added to the homepage. The Dutch drama students provided the content, based on their role performances in response to questions and warnings from the school students. Garbled and fragmented text entries added to the illusion that the material was being drawn from the past via unstable experimental technology.

As the *Timescope* element was progressively built into the project, further video footage was added to the site showing the drama students performing in as the passengers and crew of the doomed *Batavia* expedition. This edited digital video was shot naturalistically on the replica of the *Batavia*, which is a tourist attraction in the Netherlands, and in period costume. The resulting online video was dramatically framed as a 'top-secret experimental technology', the results of experimental video from the past, which were being made available to the trainee archaeologists via the Website and the *Timescope*. The children were then able to participate in an unfolding narrative partly based and driven by their own research and interests.

The final element and culmination to the project added to the Website was a longer video segment, edited from footage of the final live process drama performance at the school. This was framed as surveillance footage from the timescope experiments, showing the *Batavia* passengers and crew – drama students – interacting with the trainee archaeologists – school pupils – in real time. This in-role dialogic structure between the ANMRC trainees and the crew and passengers of the *Batavia* brought the drama to a climax in a devised live performance of the events leading to the shipwreck. The pupils and trainee researchers could activate or logon individual historical characters and question their motives and behaviour.

The barrier between the past and present became permeable until they merged in a final dramatic moment which was aided by technology. The

**Figure 6.2:** *Timescope* **video footage from the** *Batavia*

pupils who had become trainee marine archaeologists through their online research were able to question, from within the protection of the drama, the historical characters brought to life by the drama students. Ultimately the fate of the young passenger, along with many people on board the *Batavia*, was revealed in the improvised dramatic reproduction of the shipwreck and its aftermath.

The immersive development of the drama pretext, aided by the Website research, was thus paralleled by an increasing complexity in the interactivity and connectivity of the project interface. The aim of the Website was to create a pretext, a context and an environment for the drama to operate within. This was designed for the participants and not for an external audience. As Kelso, Weyhrauch and Bates (1993) point out, the performance of the users within the fictional world being created is not directed towards an audience in the real world but towards the users themselves. In the online world, as in some process drama, Interactive Drama is staged solely for the benefit of the inter-actor[s].

Beside process drama techniques the project used everyday technology such as the Website, e-mail, hypertext, Weblogs, quicktime video clips, edited digital video and live performance to develop a consensual virtual world based on a pretext that allowed the interactors to occupy two frames of reference at the same time. The use of this Web-based pretext communica-tion deliberately blurred the traditional boundaries between participant and spectator, actor and character, interactor and viewer, thus establishing a setting for process drama to occur.

Once the dramatic frame was established there was no further online 'meta-communication' (Bateson, 1972) with the pupils about the ongoing drama structure. One of the aims of the project was to use the Web-based site to build up the 'willing suspension of disbelief' to use Coleridge's (1847, p1-2) term. In drama and media practice in general there is a long history of seek-ing participatory immersion through an 'interfaceless interface' that seeks to '...erase itself so that the user is no longer aware of confronting a medium, but instead stands in an immediate relationship to the contents of the medium' (Bolter and Grusin, 1999, p8).

Process drama clearly uses symbolic material as content without any meta-communication about the process involved. Through the use of dramatic conventions the actual nature of the pretext material takes on a subjective

| Table 6.1: Symbolic alignment of digital and dramatic elements | |
|---|---|
| **Digital strategies** | **Drama elements** |
| ANMRC Website designed and built | Context established for the Pretext |
| E-mail about a mysterious letter | Anticipation of action |
| Digital photo gallery of 'trainees' | Enlistment to drama task |
| Weblogs | Establishing relationships between 'trainees' and 'marine archaeologists' |
| Digital QuickTime videos | Providing validation of effort and content. |
| *Timescope* video clips | Building tension in the drama |
| Edited video from the *Batavia* | Providing culmination for project |
| Surveillance video of live performance | Full role context |

reality that may not be readily apparent to an outside observer. A similar process of symbolic alignment was carried out with the digital pretext strategies and the drama elements as outlined in Table 6.1.

### Reflections on the *To the Spice Islands* drama project

The process of using various forms of digital connectivity as well as live performance echoes the process drama structures of O'Neill, outlined by Taylor (1995), and used to establish a pretext and conduct a successful drama. The pretext for the drama in this case included the following elements:

- Website
- an in-role presentation
- e-mail
- digital still images
- Weblogs
- QuickTime video
- edited digital video
- dialectic role-based real life performance.

The project chose to use both digital interactivity and dramatic narrativity, and deliberately tried to use hybrid performance forms to provide freedom for action as well as an immersive narrative through a pretext and digital improvisation. The structure of the project attempted to deal with one of the central paradoxes of interactive art: that action is usually prospective but story narrative is largely retrospective. Real life is never a story except in retrospect when we re-edit our experience to construct a coherent narrative for our actions. By changing the digital form used to suit the levels of commitment generated within the drama, the narrative structure was built within the dramatic frame so that action and narrative were developed simultaneously.

The essential element in this process was that the children were allocated an 'attitudinal role' (Carroll, 1988) in the fictional world of the ANMRC Website by the symbolic, linguistic and dramatic references of the pretext. The school students then used their situated role designation as trainee marine archaeologists to project themselves into the experience of the interface. This dramatic protection gave them the power to engage with the Web content and create the narrative from within the dramatic frame. The historical character performance of the adult drama students was shaped by their research into the history of the Dutch East Indiaman Company. It was also shaped by their reaction to the dialogue between their earlier ANMRC role personas as marine archaeologists, and their engagement with the pupil trainees.

Both groups of performers were engaged with the growing Website of the fictional world of the ANMRC, which contained only historically accurate information. Their analysis and input into these sources then drove the developing narrative on board the dramatic reconstruction of the world of the *Batavia*.

This developmental process occurred over a period of four weeks and produced the episodic structure that is typical of the dramatic form of process drama. Within the episodic structure there was in-role negotiation and drama and out of role research and discussion. These role switches are part of the ability expressed in all drama and provide no barrier to online dramatic engagement. Because of the dramatic conventions that had been established the pupils responded to the marine archaeologists and later to the crew of the *Batavia* with sustained dramatic involvement.

As the drama was concerned with the development of the participants' involvement, learning and change of outlook, this involvement provided some measure of validation of the effectiveness of the project. To the outside spectator the outcome of this involvement may appear somewhat undramatic as it initially consisted of mediated forms of communication. However, as demonstrated by the high level of project participation, the internal experience of the drama for the participants can be profound as the drama develops.

The reintegration of these experiences, expressed as learning outcomes for the students, was demonstrated by the quality of engagement, research and questioning evident in the culminating drama interaction between the trainee archaeologists and the *Batavia* crew. The children also demonstrated their acceptance of the transfer of digital performance elements to the live performance situation. For example, the convention of the trainee archaeologists 'logging on' to the Timescope transferred seamlessly to the live performance as a means of activating role-based performers.

Further observations of the learning outcomes were made possible by the subsequent presentation by the children of their research findings to a large adult conference audience. The children's carefully built up interactive process drama personas as trainee marine archaeologists protected them, whilst providing them with the expertise and confidence to speak and demonstrate with authority and passion about their own voyage of exploration in an online dramatic learning environment supported by a digital pretext. In this project we see the emergence of a technology-enabled/supported development of Heathcote's Commission Model, which can create a mediated learning community where students can develop real world skills from the position of occupying a situated role within a technological framework.

The potential of situated role for approaches such as serious or epistemic gaming and the Commission Model advocated by Dorothy Heathcote is further demonstrated in the second case study. This applied theatre approach uses the drama education conventions of role and pretext and applies them to the education of pre-service journalism students.

### Case study 2: The *Flood* project
### Applied theatre and technology

Definitions of applied theatre or applied drama are hard to pin down as the terms are relatively new, gaining currency in the 1990s (Nicholson, 2005, p16). Helen Nicholson argues that the terms should not be viewed in opposition to the concept of 'pure' drama as an art form or the theatre as a specialised performance space, but rather as a set of cultural and theatrical practices '...that are motivated by the desire to make a difference to the lives of others' (2005, p16).

Recently the term applied theatre has come to prominence as a general way to describe process drama that occurs outside the classroom. Judith Ackroyd describes how applied theatre practitioners are using drama in education techniques outside classroom settings:

> They share a belief in the power of the theatre form to address something beyond the form itself. So one group use theatre in order to promote positive social processes within a particular community, whilst others employ it in order to promote an understanding of human resource issues among corporate employees. The range is huge, including such as theatre for education, for community development, and for health promotion, and dramatherapy and psychodrama'. (Ackroyd, 2000, para 2)

Just as Heathcote explored 'the social condition' through her 'man in a mess' and 'mantle of the expert' approaches, applied theatre practitioners are also able to examine in a deep embodied and enacted way the issues that face the groups they are working with. In this case it was the needs of journalists to understand and respond to breaking news. The project was developed by creating an elaborate online and changing pretext. The innovative aspect of this applied theatre project is the way the pretext appears to change as the drama changes course depending on the participants.

## Artificial intelligence in drama learning

In the film *The Wizard of Oz* (MGM, 1939), the magic of the great and power-ful Oz, despite his desperate plea to 'Pay no attention to that man behind the curtain', is revealed to be technological flim-flam. This case study applies this philosophy more generally to the use of software to engage online learners in the fact that they are navigating their way through a highly complex and multi-branching, though nevertheless pre-determined, narrative. The dif-ference is that the learners are all on an individual learning journey, travelling at their own pace and interacting with the material on their own initiative.

*Flood* is a computer-delivered journalism training scenario based on the flooding of an Australian regional city. Participants take on the role of journa-lists covering the event. They are presented with information from news releases, wire service stories and sources contacted via a telephone contact book, all contained in a dedicated Website. Participants can contact sources by clicking on their phone number, which appears as a hyperlink on the page. Sources are interviewed by following hypertext links to reveal lines of pre-determined questions and responses.

*Flood* also uses freely available software artificial intelligence software, known as a chatterbot, to allow students to pursue their own line of ques-tioning through interaction with a character. The aim, like *The Wizard of Oz*, is '...to distract people away from the machinery, to make the illusion more interesting than the technical wizardry' (Murray, 1997, p219).

This is a striking example of the potential power of computers to contribute to immersive and interactive learning resources through the use of artificial intelligence (AI) software. Chatterbots are designed to operate in synchro-nous communication environments such as online chat rooms, responding to text input from human users with replies that give the impression that a real person is answering.

The software uses a series of rules to filter the input, and return a suitable reply from a database of pre-written options. There is an element of 'trickery or deception' (Wallace, 2002, para 4), but it does provide a potentially useful and powerful tool for online role-playing based on human interaction with virtual characters.

## Artificial intelligence and drama

The development of interactive narratives cannot rely solely on the setting, or the relationship of a single character, the user, to the environment; '...there must be more than one agent to create a reasonably dramatic action' (Ryan,

1997, p692). The problem for designers of interactive learning environments is the need to make characters operate at a level that will assist, rather than hinder, the user's suspension of disbelief and construction of belief.

The application of AI to interactive narrative can be seen in some of the earliest developments of computer games. Aarseth (1997, p12) notes the creation of the text-based computer adventure genre in 1976 with the release of the role-playing game *Adventure* by William Crowther and Don Woods. The game required players to type text commands, such as 'use sword', which the software would interpret and respond to. The *Flood* project, with its moderate level interactivity and branching narrative structures, can be seen to be in some ways a descendant of those early computer-based adventure games.

## Designing the *Flood* project

Journalism educators are always looking for opportunities to give students realistic experience of the working life of journalists. Patching (2002) has noted the enthusiasm with which Australian institutions channel hundreds of students into various volunteer media roles for events such as the 2000 Sydney Olympics. It is not desirable or practical to send students to every news event that comes along. There are the considerations of time, cost, safety, geography and access. There are educational concerns such as super-vision, assessment and the desire for analysis, reflection and discussion of the work being done. Hence journalism educators have long used classroom scenarios to immerse their students in their professional role and a com-munity of practice.

The *Flood* project was a training scenario designed to give tertiary journalism students experience of covering a complex unfolding story. It was based on serious flooding that affected the town of Bathurst in central western New South Wales, Australia, in 1998. Bathurst is home to Charles Sturt University and during the flooding senior journalism students worked as freelance re-porters for radio and TV news organisations. Inspired by the valuable ex-perience gained by students working on the coverage, a newswriting exercise was planned to use primary source material gathered during the flood.

The designers selected a Web delivery system, using some of the multimedia elements available including images, audio, text and video. The site attempted to marry some of the techniques and approaches of interactive game design with the aims of journalism education to produce learning materials that were more engaging for the students than the more traditional fictional paper-based exercises.

The simulation was designed around interaction with characters. Attention was paid to identifying the main sources of information, their roles in the real event and the amount and type of information they were likely to impart to journalists seeking to cover a real flood event. Video footage of the Bathurst floods was also reviewed and logged to prepare video clips for students. The students used the clips as background material so that they could see a real flood in progress, or as material for television news stories.

The fictional town of Lagoon was conceived, although its geographical situation was based on Bathurst. The designers decided to include reference to other fictional towns and localities in the region to add depth to the scenario and provide more sources of information. A map of the region was developed, as was a map of the main area of Lagoon. Place and street names were invented and added to the map. The students found a sense of the fictional geography useful when scenarios within the simulation were being conceived. It lent a geographical consistency to the simulation. The designers also decided to try to avoid any specific geo-political references in the scenario, even though it was based on events in New South Wales. They felt a generic approach might give the scenario greater value, given that it was being designed for the borderless realm of cyberspace.

The raw material gathered from coverage of the real flood provided the inspiration for the navigational features in the simulation. Background material would be provided mainly in the form of faxed media releases and wire service stories. The intention was to give students information that might help them write stories, as well as clues to possible sources of more detailed information and story angles. Some of the information would be out of date, contradictory, or generally irrelevant to a local audience as in a busy newsroom during ongoing coverage of emergencies.

The main method of pursuing story angles was via reference to the journalists' telephone contact book. Students identified the relevant organisations to contact and pursued them via the telephone contact list. Some of the organisations were obvious such as the State Emergency Service (a volunteer-based rescue organisation), Police, Fire Brigade, and The Ambulance Service. However, as the intention was to allow students to draw out a range of narratives, other elements were added, such as schools where evacuees were receiving help, local government facilities, and rescue helicopter services.

## Interaction with characters

Once the basic locations were created, a series of mini scenarios was developed to populate the artificial town with characters that would act as sources of information. The simulation uses hypertext to lead students through these mini narratives. By going to the telephone contact book or media releases, the student can locate a source of information and contact them by clicking on their phone number that appears as a hyperlink on the page. This takes them to another page for that location. These pages might contain a photo of the location. Text on the page would then inform the student of possible next steps. In some cases this might be a simple statement that the phone is not answered. In other cases the call might be answered but no opportunity is presented to interview the person who answers.

In most cases the page contains a number of hypertext links which give the student the option of pursuing a certain line of pre-determined questioning or in some cases undertaking other actions such as reading a media release. Figure 6.3 illustrates a typical page from the scenario. Students could follow these hypertext links in an effort to find all of the information that a particular character has to reveal. Some of the information would be relevant, other characters ultimately prove to be largely a waste of time in terms of the news agenda.

The designers tried to provide a mixture of responses in an effort to give variety and authenticity to the characters. Just as in reality, some characters would prove more useful than others. Some were helpful and some not so helpful. As with the media releases and other background material, some of these mini scenarios were deliberately devised as red herrings or time wasters. While the students had no choice but to pursue the lines of questioning written for the scenarios, they were still required to analyse what information was relevant or newsworthy and which story angles were worth chasing.

Finally, the designers provided navigational hypertext links to the maps of the region and a gallery of images taken during the real 1998 flood. A page providing background on Lagoon and surrounding townships was also prepared to draw students into the simulation and give them more of an understanding of the lay of the land.

### *Artificial Linguistic Internet Computer Entity (ALICE)*

In the *Flood* project it was hoped that the role of the Lagoon State Emergency Service Controller could be played by Artificial Intelligence (AI) software

○ ○                                                                     FLOOD

**HOME**

**Wires**

**Fax**

**elephone**

**Maps**

**Camera**

**Video**

bout this site
©
2001-2003
Disclaimer

A B C D E F G H I J K L M N O P Q R S T U V W X Y Z

**Lagoon Police Station**
**5555 3119**

Your call is answered:

*"Lagoon Police Station, Senior Constable Pryce speaking."*

You identify yourself to Constable Pryce.
What would you like to ask him?

- Has anything been happening overnight?
- What do you know about road closures in the Lagoon area?
- May I speak to the Duty Officer please?
- Do you know anything about a search and rescue operation near Lagoon?

**Figure 6.3: Sample page from the *Flood* scenario**

rather than relying on the pre-scripted hypertext questions. This role was modelled on a key source of information in the real Bathurst flood emergency and was a likely choice of person to interview in the simulation.

The software chosen was based on *ALICE* (www.alicebot.org), a Loebner Prize winning chatterbot designed by Dr Richard S Wallace in 1995 and subsequently refined by Wallace and others (Bush, 2001). A free hosting service (www.pandorabots.com) provided tools for creating a chatterbot and fine-tuning its responses to user input.

These chatterbots use what is called Artificial Intelligence Markup Language (AIML) to programme the chatterbot's responses. AIML provides a basic grammar for producing pattern-based stimulus-response content. In other words, it enables the chatterbot designer to create simple text files that define keywords or patterns of words and appropriate responses. For example:

```
<category>
<pattern>WHAT TIME IS IT</pattern>
<template>I'm sorry, I left my watch at home</template>
</category>
```

In this example, the <category> tag tells the software that a new input pattern and response are about to be defined. The <pattern> tag then indicates that what follows is the stimulus part of the category – the input. This is not case-sensitive, and punctuation marks are ignored. The <template> tag indicates that what follows is the response that should be given: the output.

Using this example the following text based interaction might occur:

Student:     What time is it?
Chatterbot:  I'm sorry, I left my watch at home

While this isn't a particularly enlightening response, it does make sense in the context of the question. More importantly, it does not break the illusion that the character is responding to the student's question. Most chatterbots will rely on generic default comments that can be drawn upon when all else fails. Another common approach is to change the subject, or refer to a previous topic of discussion (Murray, 1997). The main principle of this 'graceful degradation' is to avoid halting the conversation or breaking the user's willing suspension of disbelief (Ryan, 1997, p694).

During one of the trial sessions of *Flood*, the following discussion occurred between a students and the software:

Student:     What shops are damaged?
Chatterbot:  I'm just looking through our latest flood bulletin. Where did you say you where calling from?

Lacking a direct response to the input, the chatterbot software resorts to the tactic of asking the user a question. As many politicians well know, changing the subject is a good way to duck a question you can't answer. It is a good example of the *ALICE* software's primary purpose: to simulate responses so people will think they are talking to a human. But such responses may also contribute to the realism of the scenario by distracting users from the underlying technology. Murray notes that the sense of presence generated by such artificial characters '...does not come from giving factually correct information but from demonstrating dramatically appropriate behavior' (Murray, 1997, p218).

One goal for this project was to create a character students could interview who would hopefully return responses that made sense. Interestingly, even nonsensical answers might have a benefit, as they can create an air of eccentricity '... that makes the characters more memorable and lovable' (Ryan, 1997, p694) or at least seem to have a personality of their own. A small but added benefit of the *ALICE* approach is that part of the chatterbot's default database is programmed to handle some of the more obvious swear words and explicit requests that might be anticipated from users keen to push at the boundaries of the software.

## Reflections on the *Flood* project
Murray (1997) argues that one of the pleasures of digital media is the potential for immersive experiences in which we are able to construct belief, rather than just suspend disbelief. The inclusion of the chatterbot software in this project is an important step towards that experience in allowing participants to engage with a virtual character who helps them construct an understanding of the virtual world represented in the scenario. The idiosyncratic nature of most chatterbots, a by-product of the programmers' desire to deceive human users, can be exploited to engage people with the characters. There is an intrinsic game-playing nature to such software that makes it the perfect prop for people willing to play a game of make-believe with the computer (Ryan, 1997, p694).

Chatterbots pose interesting questions about the liveness of digital performance. The software is not 'a-live' as compared to human performers, but nonetheless it operates and responds in real time so that:

> ... it undermines the idea that live performance is a specifically human activity; it subverts the centrality of the live, organic presence of human beings to the experience of live performance; it casts into doubt the existential significance attributed to live performance'. (Auslander, 2002, p21)

It is this ambiguity, the difficulty in distinguishing between a live software performance and a live human performance, that makes chatterbots such a potentially powerful tool for drama and education projects incorporating online technology.

A recent example of the use of chatterbot technology to create successful online characters is a BBC-produced game based around a fictional popstar called Jamie Kane. Using a range of media including real and fictional Web-sites, the BBC created a mystery that blurred real and fictional events and resources. Players – mainly teenage girls – had to solve a series of puzzles to find clues to the fate of the missing singer. As part of the game the BBC drew upon chatterbot software to create a fictional Jamie Kane fan online chat site. The chatterbot software provided a safe environment for the teenage game players, while replicating conversations with other fans in the chat site. The software used had originally been designed to act as an online service centre for a well-known Scandinavian furniture company.

Flew (2002, p98) suggests that the development of home-based games con-soles like *PlayStation* and *Xbox* 'has drawn attention to the importance of developing media forms based around engagement and distraction, that draw the user away from 'reality' into a new thoroughly 'mediatised' space'.

A central part of this experience is the degree to which participants can shape their own experiences in the virtual world. The notion of agency is important to this project, because it highlights the possible benefits of interactive multi-media training materials compared with passive text-based resources. It allows learners to interact with the materials to draw out meaning, rather than simply being handed the information. Murray refers to agency as '... the satisfying power to take meaningful action and see the results of our decisions and choices' (1997, p126).

Traditional narratives such as theatre or cinema engage us emotionally be-cause we relinquish agency to the characters and become absorbed in the paths they take, whereas interactive digital media such as video games force us to exert agency and become the character (Perlin, 2004). This can necessitate moments where the player steps in and out of role while negotiating the mechanics of game play, such as choosing a new weapon. Similarly, some games allow players to toggle views between a subjective first-person perspec-tive and a more objective third-person view. In the *Flood* scenario students also engage with the characters at different levels. There is the more distanced hypertext-based process of following the pre-determined narrative responses or the more engaged role of interrogating the chatterbot character. This role-shifting perspective is a useful dramatic device in a learning context and a fundamental convention in process drama.

With digital training simulations such as the *Flood* package, the quality of im-mersion strongly affects the engagement of the participants. Students using the materials can readily place themselves in their commissioned roles as reporters and develop an understanding of the fictional world of the scenario.

They may have limited class or study time to become familiar with the material before being required to produce assessable work. *Flood* uses the following elements to quickly establish a simple but successful immersive narrative:

- Website populated by locations and characters with pre-determined narratives
- digital still images
- quicktime video
- chatterbot artificial intelligence software playing the role of a key character.

The project has been used with on-campus undergraduate and distance education postgraduate journalism students at Charles Sturt University. Surveys of students using the scenario have indicated overwhelmingly positive responses, a typical comment being:

> This exercise was *far, far* more exciting than any we've done this semester – it actually made me want to write the story and understand how to differentiate between important news and not so important. I found this very enjoyable!!

What the responses reveal is the power of technology and media to energise learning experiences. The changing pretext adds depth to the experience and provides potential for those interested in supporting and extending complex pretexts. Fictional scenarios and role-playing simulations are not new to journalism education but the application of dramatic principles and digital technology to create a new form of mediated learning environment has yet to be extensively explored in this area. The *Flood* suggests that the inherent strength of applied theatrical approaches can be complemented and expanded through technology. This case study indicates exciting untapped potential in marrying applied theatre approaches with appropriate technologies.

### Conclusions

These two case studies demonstrate that great potential is available to drama educators when conventional drama education approaches are transformed by appropriate and well-developed technologies. *To the Spice Islands* uses simple, commonplace technologies in a powerful way to extend and deepen the concept of drama pretext. Most importantly, through the use of technology there is now an enhancement of the traditional role in a process drama. Students can now enter a digitally-situated role and become part of a simulated, and in some cases real, community of practice. The implication is that whilst drama has always been used to teach across the curriculum with great effect in primary and secondary education, it now makes sense to use process drama approaches for all age groups. The knowledge and practices of marine archaeologists can now be accessed through the Web by students of all ages. *To The Spice Islands* enriches the learning experience by adding the distributed knowledge of the Internet and focusing it through an embodied, reflective and selective process drama.

The *Flood* illustrates that situated learning does not stop at the school gate. The integration of more complex, yet still free and accessible, technologies gives applied theatre practitioners a glimpse of what is possible when the Internet and applied theatrical approaches are combined. While the use of chatterbot technology begins to question the very nature of performance and liveness (Auslander, 2002, p21), it adds an extra dimension to what is in reality an epistemic game. Again we see a group of students operating through the enrolment process familiar to drama educators moving into a community of practice. The outcome of both of these examples is that students' learning, immersion and engagement is potentially enhanced.

Again, however, the learning experience must drive the development of the technology rather than the technology determining the learning. In both of these cases the drama was deepened and extended through the use of technologies. In *To the Spice Islands* the drama would not have been possible had it not been for the use of technology. The success of both these projects depended on the acceptance and skills of both teachers and students and the ability to accept the fiction. The potential for this strategy to reinvigorate the pretext approach will be limited only by the imagination of drama educators and their access to resources.

In the next chapter, we explore an area of drama and technology already familiar to many educators: video and television. In discussing some of the ways in which student productions can be enhanced, we consider some contemporary televisual conventions and the screen-viewing habits of the digital generation.

# 7

## Drama and screen performance

In the last five years there has been a quantum leap in the technology available to shoot and edit video. The advent of digital tools has meant that students have the resources to shoot, edit and present their own films through inexpensive DVDs. With broadband capability students can distribute through their own Websites or file-sharing computers. For some years now, Michael Anderson has marked the video drama project that is part of students' final year examinations in New South Wales and has seen significant change:

> Drama matriculation examination students have had the option over the last 10 years to develop a 5-7 minute video drama. I have worked teaching and marking several projects including performance, design and scriptwriting. While these other areas have grown in popularity and in skill, the improvements in the skills of the video makers has been truly stunning. In the early days there were videos that you would cringe all the way through. Many students produced work that had little understanding of the conventions or features of the aesthetic and no real skills in filmmaking. Typically these would be badly written 'psychological dramas' that were poorly edited and badly shot with soundtracks that were poor or non-existent.

> Occasionally one or two inspired students produced something amazing but that was the exception rather than the rule. I think this was because the area was too demanding. Students had to write, shoot and edit their films. In 1993 this was an enormous undertaking for a professional let alone a high school student.

> These students were then and are now the new auteurs. They are doing it all: writing, editing, casting and directing in a very accomplished way on consumer technology.

What I marked in 2005 showed the great progress made in the area. No longer did we have to trawl through a lot of technically inept poorly executed drama. The standard has risen. We now see in this area many professional standard video narratives that make us laugh and cry.

It is no small achievement for a 17 year-old to make a team of 'seen it all' teachers (who mark this area) react in these ways. While it is true that we are teaching the area more effectively there is also something else going on. The leaps forward in digital filming (or videoing) and editing and the pervasiveness of film literate students are making a difference to what we are seeing students make.

These students are being influenced by Tarantino and as post-modern rip; mix and burners are referencing everyone from Hitchcock to Spielberg. There are also a small number of stop-motion animators who are producing films that are witty, funny and artistically as good as many professional productions. The changes are of course about how technology makes it easier to do more, but these young people are doing more in an informed and accomplished way. This is not about only technology but the mastery of technology and the understanding of the form. I can't wait to see what they produce with the technology ten years from now.

These reflections point up the undeniable influence screened media has over our communities. The implication of this integration is that TV, the most accessible screen drama form, is not only being consumed more than any other medium but that students are now engaging actively with it, making it part of their own creative process. As Fry suggests, our consumption, appreciation and creation of screen media is now changing:

> What is clear is that television has to be recognised as an organic part of the social fabric; which means that its transmissions are no longer managed by the flick of a switch. (Fry, 1993, p13)

Television has jumped out of the box. It is no longer constrained to a particular physical form, having moved its content to a myriad of other devices such as mobile telephones, public billboards and computer screens. Television is also no longer restrained to a singular medium for discourse but rather, as Fry (1993) notes, 'the televisual' has become a cultural environment of its own. In a relatively short time it has absorbed and translated other forms, theatre, radio, film, and recombined them into television itself. (Dienst, 1994). For example, television has claimed the ground of '*liveness*', once the domain of theatre, while at the same time the development of domestic storage technology such as video, and more recently DVD, has altered our experience of 'film' (Auslander, 1999).

## Television and popularity

Why is it that when we go to a major theatre event we often meet someone we know? Not, we suspect, because we have such a wide range of friends but rather because theatre tends to attract a coterie audience. In one sense the plays of David Williamson, David Hare or David Mamet are the current versions of the masques of Ben Johnson and John Milton; they play to a select audience who have either been invited or can afford to attend and who relate to the concerns of the playwright. Television, however, attracts an enormous audience with ratings measured in millions of households. Consequently, a relatively small proportion of the population is exposed regularly to the conventions of live theatre, whereas almost everyone has a daily relationship with the conventions of television drama.

Modern media audiences are also easily able to switch into the role of content producers. The emergence of accessible and simple video-editing and capture technologies has caught theatre and by extension drama educators somewhat by surprise.

The situation for drama teachers in relation to video in school is in some ways similar to that faced by drama in relation to theatre in the 1970s. It took a long time for drama educators to work out their complex relationship with the art form of theatre. It took further time for this theory to be explained and for teaching methodology to develop into classroom practice. In the same way the relationships between the mediated drama of video and its connection to school-based work is slowly being defined.

In this chapter we consider how this developing teaching methodology comes to grips with the most pervasive of all contemporary art forms, television drama, including 'reality' programming. We'll explore the intersections of mediated performance with a drama pedagogy that is predicated on live performance and go on to explore how students use screen performances to reflect their lives and what responses drama educators can employ to facilitate and harness this interest and expertise.

## Setting the scene: reality and event television

A significant portion of contemporary television audiences are particularly captivated by what is known as 'reality' television, as illustrated in this list of the US top ten rated television programmes for 2005[1]:

1  *American Idol* (Fox)
2  *CSI* (CBS)
3  *Survivor: Palau* (CBS)

4   *Survivor: Guatemala* (CBS)

5   *Desperate Housewives* (ABC)

6   *Dancing with the Stars* (ABC)

7   *Monday Night Football* (ABC)

8   *Without a Trace* (CBS)

9   *CSI: Miami* (CBS)

10   *Extreme Makeover: Home Edition* (ABC)

This pattern of high-ranking reality and event television is mirrored in results from The UK, Europe and Australia. What is noticeable, apart from the regional programming variations, is the global trend.

Reality TV can take a variety of forms, ranging from fly-on-the-wall style observations of non-actors placed in unusual, often competitive, circumstances, through to following the daily lives of celebrities as they go about the business of being famous. Programmes encompass techniques drawn from previous television forms such as hidden camera programmes, game shows, talent quests, dating shows, soap operas, and cinema *verité* documentary. More recently, the form has become associated with what is loosely called 'event' television, characterised by allocation of significant airtime, production of related off-screen activities such as live performances, Websites, mobile telephone content, competitions, coverage of behind-the-scenes activity, heavy cross-promotion in other programmes and media and massive marketing campaigns. Audiences familiar with this style of television, which is connected to major sporting and cultural events, are now seeing similar approaches taken to lucrative reality franchises such as *Big Brother* and *Pop Idol*.

It is clear that elements of popular drama on television have evolved from live melodramas and the music halls. The open-ended series of soaps and drama that are the mainstay of free to air TV remains a strong influence on attitude and behaviour in our society and it is useful to be aware of the continuing influence of this artistic form. Just as the medieval theatre of England moved indoors and evolved into the theatre of Shakespeare, so the theatre of Chekhov, Ibsen and Scribe have moved into the mediated world of television and cinema.

Within this ongoing cultural shift towards mediated forms of drama, the wholesale adoption of the technologies of data and image capture is producing popular new dramatic forms of performance under the banner of *reality TV*. Many of these dramatic forms involve the commodification of personal and private electronic images. The images are often edited to exploit the emotional experience of individuals portrayed within them in ways that are radically different to earlier conventional concepts of role and theatrical performance.

## Reality TV as the Theatre of Surveillance

The particularly explicit form embodied in such shows as *Big Brother* and *Australian Idol* has enjoyed huge success among the youth and young adult demographic around the world. The following viewing figures provide an example of the general popularity of the form, listing the ten most watched events on Australian television this century up until February 2005[2]:

1   Tennis: Australian Open final 2005, 4.04 million

2   Rugby World Cup final 2003, 4.01 million

3   *Australian Idol* Final Verdict 2004, 3.35 million

4   *Australian Idol* final 2003, 3.30 million

5   *The Block* auction 2003, 3.11 million

6   September 11 reportage, September 12, 2001, 3.10 million

7   Wimbledon day 14, 2001, 3.04 million

8   Australian Football League grand final 2003, 2.96 million

9   *Big Brother* winner announced 2004, 2.86 million

10   *Australian Idol,* live from Opera House 2004, 2.86 million

Apart from highlighting an Australian passion for sport, and the mesmeric horror and fascination of the unfolding September 11 news coverage, the list is dominated by significant reality television 'events' (*The Block* was a home improvement reality game-show). This most popular new form of drama is what has been termed the Theatre of Surveillance (Carroll, 2002). The format covers a range of dramatic techniques and it attempts to use the centrality of electronic image capture in the culture along with unprotected role performance as a primary means of entertainment within contemporary society. Programmes like *Big Brother* and *I'm A Celebrity, Get Me Out Of Here!* fall into the reality genre of surveillance television. Every country has its own specific titles but the form is globally familiar in such shows as *Survivor, The Bachelor, Australian Idol* and *The Osbournes.*

Many of the reality event programmes in the list feature a significant live performance element. A template for these programmes has emerged, based on presenting a mixture of live and heavily edited content for most of the season, leading up to a final programme that is promoted and presented as a live performance event. The parallels between reality television and television's coverage of professional sports are probably more relevant than comparisons with other forms of television drama: they are 'highly contrived, rule-governed environments where mostly unscripted events play out' (Johnson, 2005, p92). He also argues that these programmes are often structured like a video game: a series of competitive tests, often with an unclear or ambiguous rule structure.

An analysis of these forms demonstrates that they are primarily a dramatic and artistic response to the increasing levels of mediated surveillance in western society. On average a citizen of a major industrialised city like London, Sydney or New York can expect to be captured on camera (CCTV) an estimated 300 or more times a day (McGrath, 2004, p19). Secondly, as mediated digital performance becomes ever more pervasive via Internet, DVD and satellite television, everyone has become a critic. The conventions of traditional dramatic form in film and television have become increasingly formulaic and threadbare as they did in the music hall form from which they evolved. This has led to a demand for authenticity in performance that the advent of instant capture and manipulation of digital images can satisfy.

Reality television programmes are no more representations of 'reality' than Ibsen's work was 'real' when presented on the stage of his time. Such shows are a new form of commodified cultural product, the mediatised presentation of in-role performance with its own conventions, offered up as 'authentic reality' to a new audience. Nevertheless, when combined with the interactive interface of the telephone to provide a form of audience participation, they have exerted a powerful influence on the reception of drama among young people. In the UK, the summer of 2005's most popular mobile telephone content on the Orange network was *Big Brother*, which topped 30 per cent of the audience share at its peak times at the start and end of the series[3].

*Big Brother*, as the name ironically taken from Orwell's novel *1984* makes clear, involves the surveillance and judgment of a group of young people confined in a shared house for an extended period. In Australia, although the 16-39 age demographic placed versions of *Big Brother* consistently in the top programmes in the national Oztam TV ratings surveys, other demographic groups including adults of 39 and over, disliked the show. Consistent with its popularity among the 16 to 39 age group, the programme was more popular on the Internet than it was on television. One Australian university once went so far as to block access to the show's Website, as its popularity among students was placing a strain on the information technology (IT) infrastructure.

Live video streaming via the Internet, and more recently via mobile telephones, has created a huge audience for such shows. The power of such programmes lies in their ability to interact with the audience via mobile cellphones in the voting to judge and, in the case of *Big Brother*, to eject individuals from the programme.

On another level these surveillance programmes represent an unconscious, ambiguous and uneasy response to the tensions inherent in the massive expansion of visual surveillance within our society. They represent voyeurism and embarrassment in equal measure. The private is made public and permission to stare is granted to the viewer whatever the personal price for the participants. Some research findings on these attitudes are explored in Chapter 9.

## Decoding and recoding television

Why has this hybrid form of role-based performance evolved? One possibility is that the audience for television has become aware of the constructed nature of the codes, both symbolic and technical, within which television operates. In the past many of the narrative conventions of television were accepted as given by the audience and its constructed nature was largely invisible. But with the development of video libraries, DVD technology and online behind the scene documentaries, everyone has become a critic. It has become easier to deconstruct the narratives of the industrially manufactured products of the television and film industries. Perhaps dissatisfied with the obvious narratives of sit-com and studio drama, the audience requires a return to the simulation of unmediated reality. As the narrative structure of scripted material becomes foregrounded, the shows lose their emotional appeal. The viewers have become members of 'interpretative communities', equipped with a reflexive code awareness of the genres of film and television. This has led to increasing dissatisfaction with conventional and stereotyped narrative forms but no real critique of the exploitative nature of the emerging genres.

Johnson argues that reality television is more sophisticated than many critics allow, in that it is traversing relatively unexplored territory in search of its dramatic frames and has tapped into audiences' social and emotional literacy in ways that other forms have not:

> *The Apprentice* may not be the smartest show in the history of television, but it nonetheless forces you to think while you watch it, to work through the social logic of the universe it creates on the screen. (Johnson, 2005, p99)

115

This effect multiplies when you add the participatory element of audience voting to affect the outcome of the show, as with *Pop Idol* or *Big Brother*. Viewers invest their social and emotional intelligence into the viewing experience but are uneasy about its status as performance.

So-called reality television has established a new set of codes that have not yet been deconstructed by the audience and so offers a new take on what the programme-makers term 'reality'. The focus of surveillance has intensified the mediation of the role-based performances. What the audience is getting is a simulation of unmediated reality (Goffman, 1990, p135). In Baudrillard's (1994) terms they are viewing and consuming images that are 'simulacra'; images that are constructs of an imaginary reality which is composed of dramatically-framed scenarios and attitudinal role performances.

## The drama of reality content

If we examine the dramatic structure of reality TV from a process drama perspective, what can we see? The programmes present improvised interaction dramatically framed within a drama game structure. They fail to provide any dramatic role protection for the participants within the dramatic frame. The drama is sustained through the manipulation of emotional conflict to provide a narrative structure. This constructed narrative has real consequences for the participants because the surveillance of their actions and their outcomes are unprotected by any dramatic persona and are attributed to the individual in the world outside the game show.

## What is 'real' in 'reality television'?

What is 'real' in this is the acceptance of the dramatic frame by the contestants. Once inside the dramatic frame they behave as if they are part of a new reality. The very techniques used by process drama for educational purposes are being used in a cynical exploitation of unprotected emotional response, packaged as a commodified cultural product. It is ironic that this response to a societal change in understanding how media works should produce such a culturally impoverished model of drama.

What can be learnt from the emergence of surveillance television? It is basically the commodification of a dramatic form within a mediated technology delivery system which sells the viewers the framed role performance of emotional conflict as entertainment.

Secondly, the manipulated '*real*' emotions of the participants produce not the liminal moment of theatre but only the liminoid moment of carnival and voyeurism designed for TV ratings. In contemporary mediated cultures both types of experiences coexist in a form of cultural pluralism. The liminoid experiences of media and games are a matter of choice not obligation and are often treated as a commodity and seen as fragmentary and experimental in character. The liminal experiences of theatricalised ritual or the effects of real events like 9/11, presented and shaped by television, are centrally integrated into the social fabric of the culture. Such events explore the collective intellectual and emotional meaning for all members of society connected through the mediated experience. In cultural terms, as Victor Turner (1983, p73) says, '...one works at the liminal, one plays with the liminoid'.

There has been an appropriation and blurring of different forms of 'reality' and what needs to be developed is a mediatised form of drama that transcends the technological determinism of 'reality TV' that masquerades as reality. New theatrical forms that blend the playful elements of the liminoid with the significance of the liminal, while actively engaged with the technologies of the information economy and the place of theatrical and dramatic performance within it could usefully be explored.

## Schools and screen performance
So what does this future of multi-platform delivery hold for drama and video in schools? There will be less of a gap between what people see on screens and what students in schools can produce. The use of computers and digital editing equipment means that the programmes will look increasingly sophisticated. Student comprehension of film grammar will grow with the increasing use of DVD and behind the scenes documentaries, which explore the mechanics of production. The non-linear nature of much of modern film and video will be reflected in the classroom. Non-linear story lines will increasingly reflect the high energy and concentrated dramatic structures that are now emerging in television. For example, in 1992 Channel 4 in England was showing complete four-minute dramas on prime time television. The deregulation of pay television licensing in the USA and the UK has meant that telephone companies can supply a digital signal into and out of people's homes and mobile cell phones. This led to a massive increase in the availability of new television channels, including a vast range of interactive multimedia services. This form of multi-platform media delivery, which can be loosely defined as the computer-based integration of drama, video, audio, stills and animation, is a challenging new development for drama.

Viewing television and accessing digital services, like attending school, is a cultural activity that is now a part of the dynamics of the social structure of our society. As with school, because everyone has experienced it, everyone has an opinion on television's place, value and influence within our society. Part of this general knowledge is the way people classify television genres in terms of how realistic they are perceived to be and assign a hierarchical ranking to them.

Breaking news or unscheduled major events are now commonly seen by the viewing audience as the most real, and the visual image presented on television screens or video mobile phones relays these events. This is followed by scheduled news which, though structured, has a high level of veracity for viewers. This real life image is also attributed in a modified way to the obviously constructed productions such as reality and event television, documentaries, dramas, soaps and sitcoms. But all televisual content is clearly not realistic: even breaking news is edited on the run. Realism in television is not a faithful rendition of the empirical world: it is a set of conventions by which the televisual constructs a familiar sense of reality for its audience.

It is in this common sense location of reality that television is seen as presenting an unmediated view of external reality. This view helps mask the conventions that exist within the different TV genres. These conventions are the products of the production styles that have evolved over time into recognisable genres. Television producers work hard to make the production styles they adopt appear to be the product of nature and therefore realistic, rather that a set of established conventions.

Another sense of reality exists in the televisual, namely how clearly the details of the external world are caught in the image. Real doors, real houses and real cars are juxtaposed with behavioural patterns, materialism and individuality to produce a view of the world that feels right. The external conventions of realism disguise the constructed nature of the image and the nature of the construction. Linking convention to reality makes the product appear unchangeable and unchallengeable. This is the problem teachers face when they decide to work with video. The students expect that their work will look like the constructed reality of the programmes they view on TV or, increasingly, their mobile telephones and other portable screen devices. This is especially so with drama.

An explanation of the encoded nature of television is an essential prelude to work in classrooms where television production is attempted. It is also important to be aware of the central difference between acting for the stage and for television, which relates to how the audience is positioned in each medium in relation to the performers. Actors on stage must project their characterisation to reach an audience whereas video actors must internalise their characterisation because the camera does the projection for them.

## Teaching the conventions of video drama

Student expectation about the reality of their work is often based on another common misconception about the nature of the medium which is that a television genre can be duplicated by using a different technical approach to that used by the original. What television looks like on the screen is always the result of the interaction of the genre structure and the technical equipment and infrastructure used to achieve it.

Actors in TV, more so than in film and much more so than on stage are part of the production process in which the technical constraints of the genre are more important than their acting skills. This technical structure is largely invisible to the audience who see only the effect of it in the final product. Televisual content has specific genre styles that are readily understood by everyone and parodied by television sketch comedy shows. What is not so obvious is that each of these genres has a production style that operates independently of any particular content. It is this production style that directly influences the acting style.

Therefore a sitcom like *Everybody Loves Raymond* produces stock figures that respond to a problem posed which varies from episode to episode. Soap operas like *Bold and the Beautiful, Eastenders,* and *Neighbours* have at their heart the tension of characters in inner conflict attempting to cope with outer circumstances.

A news format from any commercial network has a genre structure that sells the familiarity of the newsreader as the content, whatever the nature of the ephemeral stories they present. Reality and Event formats feature surveillance and unprotected emotional exposure as the central content of the genre.

The point is that each genre has specific technical camera conventions as well as artistic conventions, which operate to define the form:

- TV Drama and Soaps do not acknowledge the audience or the camera so a voyeuristic structure is set up for the viewer to enter. The technical conventions used are multi-camera shooting in close-up. The revelation of hidden information and how the characters react to it are the heart of the genre

■ The sitcom uses distance as the overriding convention and admits the camera and audience as existing into its world via camera laughter. The technical convention is that of forward playing in a fourth wall structure with the camera and audience on one side and the actors responding to the situation

■ The News and documentary programmes have developed their own conventions. These include the single point of view that cuts from a midshot of the presenter to a cut away of an outside broadcast story, then returns to the presenter to link with the next unrelated item

■ Reality or Event television appears unscripted but is a scenario-based framed role performance of emotional conflict, using hidden cameras to record and heavily edited responses which are combined with the game elements. What is real in this is the acceptance of the dramatic frame by the contestants and the use of game conventions.

## Making the televisual in schools

In schools only some of these technical or artistic conventions can be duplicated by relatively inexpensive domestic video camera technology. This means that any attempt to produce a realistic copy of them is bound to end in failure. The central rule is that a video acting style must be based on the production methods available. This is not so much a limitation but a freedom that releases schools from trying to look like second-rate television. Students can be taught that the conventions of emergent and short, low-budget video production differs from those of commercial TV and that the genre exists in its own right alongside but not copying these industrial production values.

What does the production style of school-based video look like? It is dependent on the limitations of the equipment and the level of editing software. Commercial video productions are often a non-linear process, with scenes shot out of sequence according to location or action and dependent on editing to produce on-screen continuity. This can be a difficult concept or process to manage with a student group. Most video cameras are capable of the following:

■ in camera editing
■ zoom
■ use of natural lighting
■ titling
■ use of fader
■ auto focus

- single camera point of view
- camera mounted directional microphone sound.

And increasingly, the use of computer-based editing software has provided a range of post-production elements including wipes, fades, titles and composite images.

This produces a style of short drama video with a range of specific conventions which have been developed by students. For example, characters often walk into shot to limit editing time and many scenes are played frontally in a fourth wall manner to accommodate a single camera set to a wide-shot. In acting terms these technical constraints need to be recognised and accommodated by the students.

The finished product often has a visual feel much like the early silent films in close up. Sound is usually poor because of lack of resources such as boom and voice microphones and this is often covered by dubbed in music tracks or non-speaking performances. This will change as technology improves. By identifying the conventions in this form they will more readily understand the parallels with the growth of the short film festival and even online short dramas.

## Using role protection to enhance student productions

The conventions of this short form of student video strips away all attempts to create non-naturalistic symbolic theatrical form. This places the acting close to the actuality of the situation whilst the adoption of role conventions still protects the students in the scene. This is a very different approach to the so-called reality genre, which offers the performers no role protection at all. Students in school uniform in a classroom look exactly that; video is brutally honest in its presentation and exposure of any pretence at shifting location or dramatic framing that is not authentic or expensively recreated. Role images that are distant from the real self of the performer appear embarrassingly dishonest when seen on the screen. The more students are directed by their teachers to 'be' a character, the less successful they usually are. Nevertheless students desperately want to 'be' characters because it offers them an in-role protection of being someone else and shields them from exposure by the camera. Unless role-protection is provided students will resort to mugging and parody, the only protection devices they know.

However the sort of screen acting possible within the technical constraints of this production style does not require the use of commercial TV or film characterisation. What is required by students acting in this special genre is the development of a role personality that uses elements of the reality of their own personality, framed within the dramatic conventions of drama in education.

When developing performance work with students in this way it is essential to find the technique to reveal authenticity rather than create a dramatic role. It is obvious that certain physical characteristics cannot be changed in video dramatisation and so must be revealed. This includes youth, gender, physical shape, and ethnicity. But the individual in role can choose to reveal aspects of themselves that are close to the dramatic image to be portrayed. This is a different approach to the usual process where a whole persona or character is assumed with outward expressions of behaviour. In student productions where this is tried this process is often accompanied by exaggerated gestures and unlikely accents.

Drama teachers are all aware of the complexity of role work and the obvious connections between drama and the roles we play in our real life that reveal different aspects of our personality. In this form of video drama the teacher helps the student performer to choose an element of themselves that is close to the role they are to play in the video whilst at the same time remaining in character.

The easiest dramatic action for video and the one that provides a sense of true role participation for the students is for the role to be a character who is playing a role. This double role structure or double intention provides an inner life for the role and encourages *listening* from others in the drama in a way that students can handle without resorting to the complexity of actor training methodology.

The essential element in this video-based dramatic style is that the performances they create must contain individuals living with the inner tension of trying to conceal their understanding of the world from those around them. A rich inner life of secrets and withheld information must be available to the performer as a basic role protection and structural device. They can always present levels of subtext to keep the inner life of the role operating. The task focus of the video then becomes the need for the participants to reveal the truth of the situation they are involved in.

Take an example of how double intention in action works in process drama on the theme of adoption. In Cecily O'Neill's *The Nature of Dramatic Action* (1988), the students were in role as children who had been sent to Australia to live in an orphanage. As young adults they returned to England to try to find their real parents. They located their parents and made contact with them but claimed to be searching for old school friends. They had to keep their real identity hidden, carry on a conversation about fictional friends and at the same time try to judge what kind of person their parent is. Could they find out why they had been sent abroad in the first place? How did their parent feel now about this action? Would this be the right moment to reveal their identity and what kind of reaction might they expect?

The precise tasks inherent in the concealment they have to perform fit the nature of the short drama video genre by providing character complexity for the performers. This style of working is similar in  many ways to the constructs of commercial video drama or soaps but the technical constraints are different. The three Rs of television: revelation, realisation and reaction, must be accommodated within the much slower pace of the single camera and the attempt at concealment of motives made by the role. The finished product often feels more like Eisenstein than a video clip. It is important to realise that this is not a fault but a *part* of the conventions that can be learnt and understood by the students. Acting in this form of video consists of revealing, while trying to conceal the motives adopted in the role that come close to aspects of the student's own character. This dramatic structure protects the students and paradoxically allows truth in performance in a way that the commercial forms of reality TV rarely can.

## Conclusions

The use of much in-role performance and interactivity as seen in reality TV is the theatrical form drama teachers seem uniquely positioned to provide and critique in drama classes. It may be that through their artistry and use of process drama conventions they are able to provide access to authentic physical performance in a way that the voyeuristic forms of reality TV avoid. Drama teachers using dramatic conventions are able to provide the authentic moment of drama participation for their classes rather than the constructed moment of carnival and voyeurism driven by television ratings, that surveillance or reality TV provide. The drama curriculum operating in schools using video should be able to help young people construct a sense of identity that will aid them in their collective agency and self-determination, and provide understanding of the conventions of the currently popular commodity forms of theatre exemplified through commercial televisual performances.

In the next chapter we examine how teachers can use similar processes to understand and harness video games in the drama classroom. We discuss the recent interest in games for learning and suggest some applications for drama education of video games.

## Notes

1 Nielsen ratings, reported in the New York Post < http://www.nypost.com/entertain ment/60402.htm>

2 As reported in the *Sydney Morning Herald*, February 3, 2005 <http://www.smh.com. au/articles/2004/03/30/1080544476965.html?from=storyrhs>

3 According to figure released by Orange at http://www.prnewswire.co.uk/cgi/news/ release?id=155257

# 8

## Drama conventions, video games and learning

ave you ever dreamt of creating a best-selling novel, a hit Broadway play or a blockbuster film? If you want public acclaim and global celebrity, these can be your goals to aim for but if you want massive audiences and huge financial rewards, video game production should be your aim. The games industry, including computer games and proprietary consoles such as *XBox, PlayStation* and *GameBoy*, now outstrips other forms of box office in many countries. The production budgets for many new games rival the million dollar ventures behind major cinema releases. The number of paying monthly subscribers to online games increases by thousands every month. The reality is that only a small percentage of game titles make the bulk of the profits: the rest struggle to break even. But the smash hit titles not only make money in off the shelf sales but also in cross-over products. Increasingly, popular game titles are making the switch to movies, toys and other off-screen merchandising (eg *Tomb Raider, Resident Evil* and *Doom*), exploiting their own dramatic properties.

The video game is one of the most obvious forms of technology to pervade popular culture in recent years. In the space of three decades, video games have become a multi-billion dollar global industry to rival the net takings from other media forms such as book publishing and movie-making. Not surprisingly, given the dramatic developments in connectivity and multimedia capabilities of these products, there has been a wave of interest in the more purposeful application of this technology to the classroom or training environment. This has been accompanied by attempts to develop theoretical methods of analysing video games and to justify them as objects worthy of academic study.

There is resistance to the 'serious' treatment of video games as a learning and performing tool in classrooms. Their development has long been dogged by concerns over violence, gender bias and portrayal of anti-social activities. It is certainly true that negative themes can be found in many popular entertainment games but the relative merits of particular titles are not our concern. Video games as a form of experiential media provide a new space for the development of powerful mediated learning communities and potential new performance spaces.

This chapter looks at the similarity between the conventions of the live role-based performance of process drama and the mediated performance within role-playing video games. Consider the following statements by two influential exponents from the fields of educational drama and video game-based learning respectively. First, Dorothy Heathcote:

> I am concerned in my teaching, with the difference in reality between the real world where we seem to 'really exist' and the 'as if' world where we can exist at will. ... It is the nature of my teaching to create reflective elements within the existence of reality. (Heathcote, 1991, p104)

And James Paul Gee writes:

> They [video games] situate meaning in a multimodal space through embodied experience to solve problems that reflect on the intricacies of design of imagined worlds and the design of both real and social relationships and identities in the modern world. (Gee, 2003, p48)

As these practitioners point out, both process drama and video games deal with the shifts in identity formation that are possible within an imagined or virtual environment. This playing with identity is particularly evident in the way that the presentation of the self in the online environment is coded as mutable and capable of growth and increase in status. In process drama the exploration of the relationship between identity and power is a defining characteristic of the form (Carroll, 1988). This experimentation with identity and power expressed within the parameters of a video game or a process drama session may challenge traditional notions of a central or essential identity, especially in the context of race, class and gender through the adoption of alternative dramatic roles.

The mutability or morphing of a constantly reinvented identity provides a new metaphor for connecting the episodic nature of in-role performance and out-of-role reflection in both drama and video games. These social constructionist notions emphasise the spatial and temporal locatedness of identity

(Hall, 2000). Rather than being fixed, identities are seen as 'necessary fictions' (Weeks, 1995) or '... points of temporary attachment to the subject positions which discursive practices construct for us' (Hall, 2000).

## Situated role and powerful identities

In presenting a case for video games as a means of transforming education, Shaffer (2005) notes that the virtual worlds created in epistemic games can provide a learning space where 'learning no longer means confronting words and symbols separated from the things those words and symbols are about in the first place'. Thus the laws of gravity can be understood through a virtual experience of walking on different planets, rather than through analysis of an equation. Epistemic games allow players to develop situated understanding, and to experiment with new and 'powerful identities'. This is similar to the principle of situated role we have described as a possible outcome of the transformation of process drama through technology and media.

The concept of enacted role and temporary identity, explored within the process drama field so thoroughly by Heathcote (1991), Boal (1995), Bolton (1998) and others, can be applied to provide an analysis of the dramatic role possibilities of multiple identity play in drama and in interactive games environments. The closeness of performance elements within both fields can be seen as an adaptation of dramatic role to the changing cultural forms being generated by gaming platforms, interactive networks and developing online digital media.

The field of identity formation that both drama and video games encompass means they are uniquely positioned to grapple with this issue in a cultural climate of increasing openness and identity relativism. Process drama is able to provide a positive idea of the place of the individual in post-structuralist thought by providing drama conventions that negotiate constantly shifting identities. Within process drama the participant can be seen as a subject-in-process, capable of agency, role differentiation and integration within a range of environments, both digital and dramatically enacted, that replicate the mulitmodal discourse of that long standing semiotic signing system: the theatre.

As Heathcote says, '...the theatre is the art form that is totally based in sign' (1991, p169). In the past a single mode – usually text or icon – of communication was the only form available in the digital world (Carroll, 2002). But digital technology has made it possible for one person to be engaged in all aspects of multimodal immersion and production. In the past this character immersion was usually the preserve of the trained actor or the participants in role-based process drama.

As authors such as Turkle (1997, p184) have pointed out, such role-based digital involvement may not be all fun and games – there may also be important identity work going on as there is within process drama role taking. Such role immersion used to be preceded by extensive training for actors to clarify the distinctions between identity and role. Untrained individuals were guided by directors or skilled teacher/facilitators in process drama, whereas in video games induction may be limited to the cinematic cutscenes and introductory narrative.

Turkle's argument suggests that while some individuals may use cyberspace to express dysfunctional offline selves, most use the digital domain to exercise and experiment with what might be considered truer identities. Maybe it is here that the first collaborations of the digital world and drama classroom could occur.

Other cybercultural critics have been less optimistic. Nakamura (2000) suggests that rather than any kind of radical performance, this identity tourism involves the act of playing the fantasy Other, so reaffirming rather than challenging real life stereotypes. This seems to be the case with the gender boundaries in *EverQuest*, *Diablo* and other online games.

## Open texts: A case study of *EverQuest*
Whatever the pros and cons of this radical 'stepping into another's shoes' (Heathcote, 1969), the connection between the conventions of process drama and immersive digital role-playing is even stronger when considered in terms of semiotic production. Because both forms exhibit the multimodal 'open text' described as characteristic of contemporary communication, both are oriented towards the semiotic action of production. As Kress points out, the screen is now the dominant site of texts; it is the site which shapes the imagination of the current generation around communication (2003).

As Eco puts it, the author or composer, artist, playwright, instructor or game designer offers a work to be completed by the reader or listener, viewer, performer, student or player, such that 'the common factor is a mutability which is always deployed within the specific limits of a given taste, or of predetermined formal tendencies' (1989, p20). A work can be offered as a 'plastic artifact' which can be shaped and manipulated by its audience but which still operates within the world intended by the author. Eco defines a subcategory of open work, the 'work in movement', which Aarseth suggests is the closest link to interactive media forms because it is built upon unplanned or incomplete structural elements, allowing a process of mutual construction to occur (Aarseth, 1997, p51).

An environment where the conventions of the open text forms of both process drama and video games can be compared is Sony Online's *EverQuest* (http://eqlive.station.sony.com/). This is a massively multiplayer online role-playing game. Thousands of players can be active at the same time and can share the same game world in real-time. The world of *EverQuest* is a 3D graphical environment populated by players' avatars in the form of humans, elves, gnomes or even beasts: these characters take on roles such as ranger, druid, wizard or warrior. The combinations of races and roles produce game characters with different skills in a range of areas from combat to magic, and healing to crafts. Players may simply explore the vast game world and deal with the events and characters they encounter or they can engage with various quests or missions that are part of the game design. Players can communicate via text-based chat tools built into the game interface, and they may form alliances to tackle a quest as a group by pooling specialist skills and abilities. Social interaction, either as *ad hoc* encounters or more formally structured as questing parties or guilds, is part of the game's appeal.

The texts of both process drama and video games demand constant interpretation and articulation. As Gee (2003, p11) suggests, in role-playing games you can design your own character, and this is also true of process drama. Both forms exhibit the episodic form that alternates in-role behaviour with out of role activity. For example, in the video game *Diablo*, after completing a task in character role, the player as player returns to the armory to buy upgraded weapons before returning to role performance with enhanced powers.

In drama and games there is the alternation of in-role enactment and out of role negotiation, along with research, discussion and planning. Table 1 (page 130) matches some of the obvious similarities between these two forms.

When entering the dramatic frame in both process drama and video games 'a willing suspension of disbelief' (Coleridge, 1907) is established. In the case of drama this is through the negotiated agreement of the participants and its formalising by the facilitator, often using narrative as a focus. Video games have a similar formal narrative often expressed in cutscenes and narrative overlay, which establish the dramatic world. Often instruction or guidance is provided by characters within the narrative and dramatic frame of the game. This function operates as teacher-in-role in drama and commonly as a

**Table 8.1: Comparison of process drama and video games**

| Process drama | Video games |
|---|---|
| Group narrative orientation | Video intro/cinematic cutscenes |
| Teacher in role | Instructions from superior, helper etc |
| Discussion of role attributes | Selecting role attributes |
| In-role, attitudinal drama | In role, playing 'as if' a character type |
| Out of role research | Handbook, cheats, history |
| Learning activity focus | Speed challenges, custom games |
| Building role (costume, props etc) | Inventory and attribute building |
| In role, character | In role, experienced character |
| Discussion, debrief | Online chat, Web user groups |

superior, as in rank or status, or helper, in video games. Out-of-role tasks that occur are part of the activity, like selecting role attributes or engaging in research. As well as these activities there are different levels of playing involvement in both dramatic forms as well as out of frame discussion.

*Role distance and role protection*

The concept of the dramatic frame is clearly operating in video games such as *EverQuest*, where the player is engaging 'as if' the situation is real (Goffman, 1974) but where a range of conventions vary levels of protection for the player. The player can toggle between a close identification with their character and a observer/learner perspective that is more distant and willing to experiment at extreme levels to discover how to operate within the game environment. Often, as with *EverQuest*, novice players suffer little or no penalty for failure in the early stages of a game.

This penalty-free behaviour reflects what psychologist Eric Erikson (1968) has called a psychosocial moratorium, which James Gee (2003, p62) succinctly sums up as '... a learning space in which the learner can take risks where real world consequences are lowered'. In *EverQuest* high-risk behaviour is sometimes rewarded on early skill levels. For example, one of the authors learned to take advantage of the *respawning* that occurs when a character dies, such that if he got lost or trapped in a difficult location he would deliberately kill off his character by drowning or attacking a much stronger foe. His character would then be returned to a familiar location without major penalty, that is without loss of treasure and equipment. Similarly, he learned that attacking creatures of similar or higher skill level was a risky enterprise but even if only occasionally successful in these battles a player can accumulate experience points more quickly as a reward for defeating a strong foe. While learning to play, 'death' is an inconvenient but acceptable penalty for pushing the boundaries of the game.

In process drama this concept has come to be known independently as 'role protection', where the personal distance from the consequences of actually being in the event have been elaborated and structured for different learning outcomes. This role-protection or psychosocial moratorium can be seen in a metaphorical way as an interface that frames the dramatic and performative event. Previously this frame was seen as a picture frame or proscenium arch framing the action. More commonly today it is the screen frame of the computer that performs that function.

This frame acts as a border separating the images and events from those in role protection. The participant enters this framed world with a mutable identity based on parameters of the performance role available to them. By focusing attention on the performative actions within the frame it clearly delineates the difference between real life and the representation of reality we call role-based video games or process drama. This is the 'as if' device which provides the dramatic role protection that allows the participants to enter the space of enactment.

This performance form is composed of two elements: the nature of the conventions operating on the screen or within the drama and the level of role protection or role distance to allow the adoption of a new identity within the penalty-free area of the dramatic frame.

Figure 8.1 shows these elements in a less metaphorical way:

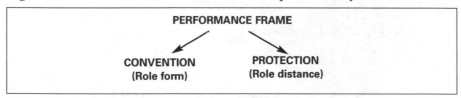

**Figure 8.1: Elements of the performance frame**

The conventions operate as creative forms for both video games and process drama by developing non-naturalistic ways of presenting material and adapting roles within the performance frame. Within process drama this covers a range of positions including attitudinal role, signed role and character performance, as well as more abstract forms such as effigy, portrait, statue and narrative voice (Neelands and Goode, 2000). Within video games the player has a similar range of positions from first-person shooter to central character, controller and interactive performer. These conventions are built into the performance frame and provide the structure for the fictional social world to exist.

There is also the protection of role distance that allows the psychosocial moratorium to operate for the participants within the performance frame. In stand-alone video games it is the penalty-free nature of the interaction that constantly allows the character to learn by mistakes. However, while providing high levels of role distance and role protection, stand-alone video games still allow participants to experience the performance frame from alternate positions. For example, in the real-time strategy game *Starcraft*, the player can control any of three different species, Terran, Protos or Zerg, each with its own unique goals, technologies and abilities. In massively multiplayer online games like *EverQuest* the penalties associated with avatar death may be much closer to those of situated role in a mediated process drama than non-networked or single-player games.

In a more metaphorical way the Performance Laptop in Figure 8.2 illustrates these points. The laptop frame provides the space and performance conventions for a distanced performance and operates for both drama and video games.

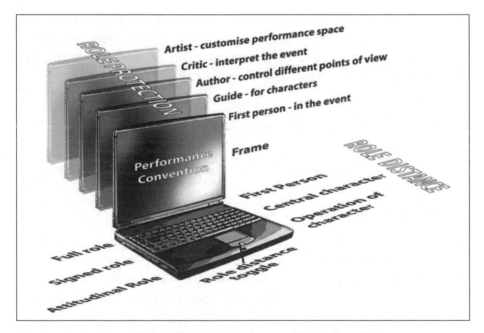

**Figure 8.2: The Performance Laptop, illustrating role distance and role protection**

The player/performer always has the option to select from a range of distance and protection conventions. The most obvious position is immersion in the action of unstructured first-person participation. This full role, first-person shooter (FPS) position, while providing high levels of involvement and activity, provides minimal levels of protection for the participants. In video games, FPS game forms are often based on reflex action and physical controller skills and depend on an ever-growing body count of increasingly ferocious adversaries for success. In other more quest-based video games such as Nintendo's *Zelda* series, the first-person view is more open and problem-based, and much closer to the drama concept of full role.

Within process drama, first-person full role and immersion in the event is usually the culmination rather than the starting point of any improvisational drama. First-person 'in-the-event' drama requires a background understanding of the context and high levels of group trust to operate in a situation with minimal role protection.

If this minimal role distance is overly confronting the participant/player can choose a greater role distance within both forms and stand back from the action by the assumption of an attitudinal role. This maximally distanced role requires only the agreement of the player to take on an attitude of a character in the drama for it to operate. An *EverQuest* player could choose to ignore the connected aspects of the game, avoiding communication with other players and pursuing their own intra-game pursuits, such as mapping the game world. They could imbue their character with a desire to observe the game world, rather than interact with it.

At a role distance closer to the action, the player can become a central character by signing the role they have adopted through costume, name, career path or some other attribute. They can actively engage other human players, adopting a particular tone in their text-based conversations to convey a deeper sense of their role. At the role distance level closest to being-in-the-event, the player can assume a full role and become part of the unfolding narrative action. The role distance chosen is always variable, and the player can toggle between levels of involvement in a video game through changes of camera perspective. Sometimes this is for a strategic reason, to get a larger picture of what is happening but sometimes it is because the emotional closeness of the action becomes overwhelming.

This first-person full role is, as we saw, the most emotionally exposed position. But the player can choose to maintain a full role but stand back somewhat from the moment of unstructured participation by becoming a guide for the character, or an author of the narrative. In *EverQuest*, a player can choose to 'hire' other players to complete a difficult or dangerous task, rather than attempting it themselves. Similarly, a player can choose to develop their character as a service provider, such as a healer, tailor, fletcher, blacksmith or minstrel to other players, rather than participating in the game's pre-designed quests. These roles are often presented as non-player characters or software controlled agents, but human players can take on these roles if they wish.

Similarly, within process drama the teacher/facilitator may shift the role distance of the participants in a group enactment if the level of role protection does not provide enough artistic distance from the dramatic intensity of the event.

Both the performance forms, unlike real life, mean that the participants are not trapped in the present moment of unstructured participation. The performance frame for both drama and video games allows the participants to structure the protection of role distance that is appropriate for their needs.

The performance frame, the conventions and the levels of protection are shown in a metaphorical way in Figure 8.2 above. All of the levels of protection and varieties of convention are available on any piece of work.

Of course the ultimate protection for both drama and video games is to exit the performance frame altogether, and this episodic quality is part of the dramatic form: most games feature a pause function. However, the combination of role protection and role distance from the focus event provides the dramatic structure that protects the participants in their dramatic involvement with the narrative.

All varieties of role distance are performative, and distanced roles are often used in drama but less so in video games. With drama, participants feel more protected and work with more conviction if they are framed at some distance from the moment of real time enactment. If too much is at stake, the role distance is often too close for an exploration of the situation, and the performance frame becomes blurred while the belief in the convention and protection of the role is lost. In video game genres, role distance varies. In first-person shooter forms, the visual rush of imminent destruction often drives the action. In other quest-based games a more reflective position is available.

### Player perspective, role distance and role protection

One way to explore how the dramatic conventions of role distance and role protection apply in video games like *EverQuest* is to consider the screen views available to the player. Following a video game convention of equating player perspectives and role distance with 'camera views', the player can cycle through the options to choose to view the game from different angles, and also zoom in or out and pan left and right using keyboard commands. Table 8.2 outlines the camera views offered in *EverQuest*.

| Table 8.2: The camera views in *EverQuest* | | |
|---|---|---|
| **Description:** | **View:** | **Camera position:** |
| First-person (default) | Straight ahead | Player cannot see character |
| Overhead (rotating) | From above | Rotates as character turns |
| Rear (rotating) | From rear | Rotates and stays behind the character |
| Overhead (fixed) | From above | Does not rotate as character turns |
| Rear (fixed) | From rear | Does not rotate as character turns |

In practice, we found that playing the game comfortably and efficiently required a constant process of toggling between the first-person view, a view from over the shoulder of the avatar, and a distant third-person view. The 'ideal' view depended on the task being performed. For example, we found a first-person view good for navigating through corridors in pursuit of another character, while switching to a third-person view was sometimes necessary in a melée fight to ensure the avatar wasn't being attacked from behind.

As noted in Figure 8.2, a first-person perspective in terms of both role protection and role distance is the most likely to equate with a sense of being within the action; it is 'as if' you are the character. First-person view is the most 'real' perspective available in this game, and in others like it. Indeed, the 'first-person shooter' is recognised as a game genre in itself, modelled on neo-classics such as *Doom, Quake* and *Unreal*. It is the perspective that most places the player in the skin of the character avatar. The world is seen through the character's eyes. The point-of-view afforded the player in video games is often discussed in terms of immersion, the degree to which the player is drawn into the mediatised reality of the game environment.

Other camera positions offered in *EverQuest*, as listed in Table 8.2, present options for varying degrees of role distance and protection as outlined in Figure 8.2. Whenever the player is in role, standing apart from the action and looking down on their avatar, this role distance brings highly affective subjective elements into the social relationship being negotiated (Kress, 2003, p118). The player is always in control of the role distance they choose. It is their desire for engagement that dictates how close to the naturalistic frame of total involvement they will go. These conventions exist as a visual genre which is similar in form to the illustrations that exist in a multimodal text as outlined by Gunter Kress in *Literacy in the new media age* (2003, p118). The distance and positioning of the viewer in any visual text, video game or drama is always critical to their role position. Like many games, *EverQuest* allows the player to quickly toggle or cycle through camera position using keyboard commands. In this manner role distance can be changed more quickly and more often than is usually the case with process drama.

Figure 8.3 illustrates the third-person view in *EverQuest*. Here the authors, in the guise of their character Elviss the Ranger, have been attacked from behind by a Restless Skeleton, a computer-controlled character. The authors have toggled from first-person to third-person perspective to quickly gain a sense of the melée. In terms of role distance, this is a mid-range engagement that is in the action but not too close for comfort. Being able to assess the situation and plan a response in third-person view is less distressing than reacting to an attack from a seemingly invisible enemy in first-person view.

Note that *EverQuest* intrinsically acknowledges that sometimes players want to shift to other role frames during the game. One of the communication modes afforded in the game is known as '*out of Character*' chatting. By typing

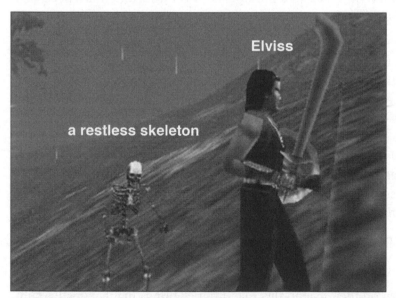

**Figure 8.3: Third-person (rear rotating) view in *EverQuest*. Attacked from behind, the authors have adopted this perspective/role distance to identify their foe and plan a response**

136

in 'ooc' mode, a player speaks out of character to all nearby players. The game instructions describe this facility as being '...for speaking out of the context of the game and your character'. An odd but amusing example of this is shown in this transcript of text-based conversation, in which the character of Bareback comments out of character about Elvis's name:

Bareback says, out of character, Love me tender, love me sweet

Elviss: Do you like my hair?

Bareback: Yes I do

Elviss: I would like my shoes to be blue suede

Bareback: That would be cool

This ability to toggle social interactions instantly and explicitly in and out of character clearly allows for shifts in role protection. This exchange equates to the role protection frame of critic, who can interpret and comment on the action. This level of spectatorship is highly protected and a long way from first-person involvement. Indeed, it is often the functional aspects of gameplay that afford the ability to alter levels of role protection. The player can choose to be in the action as a first-person participant or they can switch to the more protected role of critic by choosing to communicate out of character.

An even more protected position is that of the artist customising their experience. In *EverQuest*, this is typified by the function of allocating accumulated skill points to selected areas to enhance a character's ability. In this mode the character is not perceived as an avatar, but as a table of skills and abilities that can be favoured or ignored, depending on how the player wishes to shape their experience. In video and computer games more generally, this high level of role protection is found in the practice of modifying the game code or in creating new game levels or scenarios using software tools and programming skills.

## Process drama, video games and learning

Learning concepts drawn from process drama, such as understanding role distance and role protection (Carroll, 1986), apply closely to video games learning. For example, by initially ignoring a game's manual, most players appear to have a learning experience that closely mirrors the process of experiential learning that occurs in role based process drama (Cameron and Carroll, 2003). In the role-playing video game *EverQuest*, a player's continued interaction with game elements and tasks is rewarded with points for experience. A new player practices martial skills by killing rats, skeletons and other creatures that conveniently exist in plague proportions on the introductory levels. By becoming successful at these tasks the character is eventually promoted to a higher skill level. Each time a character is promoted, the player can distribute a small amount of experience points among a range of character skills and attributes. In this way the player can shape the character's growing expertise in or knowledge of certain areas.

*EverQuest's* promotion system also allows for a penalty-free learning zone for the player. Until a character is promoted to a skill level of ten, they can die and be re-generated largely without loss. They will be returned to a safe location, and will keep whatever items they were carrying at the time. However, once a character achieves level ten experience, it becomes necessary for the player to locate their 'corpse' in order to recover those items. If the character has died in a particularly awkward location, recovery may not be possible. This can be a significant penalty in a game that relies heavily on the collecting of powerful weapons, useful tools, valuable objects and magical items. Maintaining this inventory can be an expensive pursuit, both in terms of accumulating the game wealth to purchase or pursue these items, and literally in terms of the subscription costs to play the game long enough to develop a character's worth.

Restricting the risks for characters below level ten experience allows new or less able players to indulge in high-risk behaviour while at the same time being protected by their role distance from deep identification with the character so that their potential danger becomes a positive learning experience. We have noted a similar process at work when learning to play other video games, such as their introduction to *Resident Evil – Code: Veronica X* that frequently involved gruesome deaths for their avatar Claire, the character representation of the player, until their skills and strategies improved (Cameron and Carroll, 2004).

## Conclusion

There is already considerable discourse on the developing forms of digital interactive drama. Our contribution to that discussion is the theoretical connection between the conventions of live role-based performance of process drama and the mediated performance of online role-playing video games. It is clear that a central element of both process drama and multiplayer online video games is their ability to allow participants/players to 'step into somebody else's shoes'. Both forms contain role distance and role protection conventions that allow fluid toggling between close active engagement in the unstructured moments of the event, and a more protected observation or reflection on the experience. In video games, this toggling can be as instant as a keyboard press to switch the on-screen viewing perspective.

Our experience in learning to play *EverQuest* demonstrates the increasing closeness of performance elements within both fields. Process drama's appeal in the educational setting is its ability to provide a protected means of exploring curriculum learning from an experiential position. The mutability of digital identities, as realised in online games, provides a similar penalty-free opportunity for exploring social relationships, identities and experiences 'as if' the player is somebody else. Switching in and out of or between characters or toggling distance between first-person participation and third-person observation, provide mechanisms by which the participant/player can reflect on and adjust their involvement in the events they are a part of.

The challenge inherent in the digital gaming form is to explore how this connection might be applied in fields such as education, where western young people's concepts of performance, role and individual identity have already been changed by an increasingly mediated world. The ability to manipulate or edit identity is a concept already assimilated into the digital world view of many young learners. As more video game-based resources for the classroom emerge, it becomes increasingly important to incorporate artistic notions of role distance and role protection in their development. This may also help to address the moral panic reactions to the use of games in classroom learning.

Continuing discussion is essential between educators, process drama specialists and game designers on how best to connect these new learning and identity conventions with artistic form and curriculum content.

# 9

## Researching Emerging Practice

### Introduction

Technology is a huge area at the moment for teachers. I am lucky to be computer savvy, but I have learnt that from muddling my way through myself with computers. When I arrived at university I didn't know how to turn a computer on!

Kids are so used to being instantly satisfied in the most amazing ways – they turn on the TV and are bombarded with images that even the wildest imagination couldn't create. They have the *Xbox, PlayStation* and computer games. They don't need to create their own drama or entertainment because everything is instant in their worlds. Learning is something that kids need to be motivated to do. How you motivate your class becomes a very personal thing – connecting to technology, but it is something that is constant and is ongoing. (Lauren, a newly graduated Australian teacher, 2005)

M any teachers constantly review and adapt the way they teach to connect with the digital natives in their classroom. They shape, re-fine, test and modify their approaches to teaching. This may not be a deliberate strategy; for many it is simply the way they work. If one approach fails, try another until a suitable method is found. This is a dynamic process of research and practice: all educators are informal researchers. No class, lesson or student is exactly the same as another. From one year to the next, the students, syllabus, texts, trends and ways of teaching change, and teachers regularly try new approaches. Some educators call it evaluation of emerging practice and reflection; some call it research.

This chapter seeks to encourage educators and practitioners to consider how their own stories, experiences, experiments and performances might contribute to further understanding and investigation.

We begin by sharing some of our personal experiences of researching the intersections of drama, education and technology. This is not a definitive coverage of the research possibilities in the area nor is it a comprehensive how to. The intention is to provide insight into the work that preceded this book and to the conclusions we draw about the potential new worlds for learning and performance.

## Positioning drama and technology research

Drama educators work on the fringes of school curriculum. Being a fringe dweller has its disadvantages. Drama educators are often the last to receive resources, as mainstream curriculum areas push them to the periphery. However, there is much to be gained from the fringes. Drama educators can see the centre from where they stand and make informed choices about how their work will be distinctive from mainstream education. Students who do not fit in to traditional models of schooling come to drama to find a home. The tension and stimulus of fringe dwelling comes from fighting for your existence and watching your students work with a powerful and rigorous art form.

Being on the fringe can also make for exciting research because we can apply innovative methods to the content of our research. If drama education research had a fringe area it might be technology. There are so few active researchers in the area, so little research available and such deep-seated teacher – and presumably researcher – mistrust (Flintoff, 2002a, p191). But there is also a real interest and desire to integrate the technological world of their students into one's own teaching. At an international drama conference in 2004, over one hundred teachers and researchers joined a special interest group convened to research into drama and technology (International Drama and Education Association, Ottawa, Canada). Nevertheless, drama teachers are justifiably sceptical about educational technologies that are promoted as educational solutions.

What is clear is that there is demand from students to explore ways for the liveness of the drama learning experience to be enhanced and supported by technology. Research has not reported on current practice and has tried to form and describe drama education's future. Teachers working within the field of drama and technology are not yet supported by a body of research or sets of theoretical principles to guide their practice. There is little understanding of the area, and while there are many who value the idea of tapping into contemporary youth culture, few practitioners have the time or the energy to try new approaches.

Drama and technology research has been developed from the technology side rather that the drama side, with groundbreaking works such as *Computers as Theatre* (Laurel, 1991) and *Hamlet on the Holodeck* (Murray, 1997), but the insights of drama especially role-based process drama – have not been fully considered. There is an urgent need to present the case for the integration of orthodox drama with technology and to make new theory to serve drama education's future. The urgency of this call to research should not be underestimated; it is as serious as Philip Taylor's call a decade ago to make research the basis of drama education's fight for legitimacy (1996, p3):

> If a central aspect of arts education is the new light that is shed on the moment or the event, or a different understanding provoked by the work ... how can teachers take risks with their students and thereby honour the artistry encountered? If arts worlds are about the possible world we can enter and the virtual realities exposed, how can research probe and liberate?

In this chapter, we each try to respond.

## Some questions about methodology and pedagogy – Michael Anderson

The central question for me in drama, technology and education is: how can technology make the live experience in classrooms and theatre more effective for young people? The most important role for research in this area is to examine whether there are new ways for young people to express their creativity through technological tools. The landmark *The Arts and Education: New Opportunities for Research* supports this approach and nominates further areas requiring research:

> New technologies have led to the creation of new artistic media and forms. To date, little research has explored the particular cognitive and physical demands and possibilities inherent in work in these new media. Further research might be done to explore the consequences of pursuing work in these new media and forms. ... As technologies are adapted and discovered, and as new uses for available technologies are devised, researchers might find further grist for work pertaining to the arts. (Arts Education Partnership, 2004, p19)

Away from advocacy and promotion, drama education research related to technology must ask probing questions such as:

- What benefits do students derive from using technology in the drama classroom?
- Who is left behind in the learning when technology is used ?

■ How does drama teaching and learning change when technology is introduced?

■ Can digital natives use technology to transcode live dramatic properties into digital applications?

■ How are the aesthetics of drama education and performance changed by technology?

■ How does technology support the development of situated role?

■ How can epistemic games be applied to drama learning?

■ What potential does the Commission Model have for online learning?

■ How can serious gaming interact with traditional process drama approaches?

■ Why are teachers sometimes reluctant to introduce technology into drama learning?

A thriving drama education research culture is evident in two publications by John O'Toole and Judith Ackroyd due in 2006. Building on the wealth of emerging drama education research is the most effective way to develop the research. While drama researchers work with methodological approaches, it is case studies, arts-informed and practice-based approaches which provide potential for educators to examine and communicate their work.

## The development of rich case studies in drama and technology

A case study is a useful methodology for research in drama and theatre education grounded in the natural setting of the drama activity. It is a familiar and well-used approach to drama educators (Bolton, 1996, p190). There has also been a call from technology educators to use case studies to report theory and practice (Foster, 2002, p42) which suggests that when developing understandings in technology education case study is a natural choice:

> Case study analysis is only an appropriate educational research model for a limited range of research questions, specifically those in areas of education where foundational questions remain unanswered. It is clear from the literature that technology education is such a field. Several of the most respected technology-education researchers have identified large domains in which little or no quality research exists, and have pointed in general to the need for more qualitative research to fill these voids.

Drama educators have seen strong advances in the development of research over the last decade which has largely been due to teacher researchers in the field using qualitative and often case-based methodology to interrogate drama learning. Foster's (2002) call for foundational understandings is required in drama education but most acutely in the emerging area of drama and technology.

Case study fits our needs because drama, by its very nature as a negotiated group art form, is a non-reproducible experience. The participants in a drama or theatre education session create a unique set of social relationships that become a single unit of experience capable of analysis and study. Because of the complexity of the interactions, the whole creative sequence needs to be studied, not just aspects of variables within it. These characteristics are also aspects of a case study methodology (Hartfield, 1982) and provide a close fit for drama researchers to follow.

Case study data is useful when the researcher is deeply involved in the structures, processes and outcomes of a project, particularly so when the researcher is operating inside the group using dramatic role conventions (Neelands and Goode, 2000, p5) which frame the constructed world of the drama. Case study methodology allows examination of the social action of drama in its negotiated and framed setting in an open and flexible manner. It can interpret the nature of power structures and the interaction of the participants within them.

Finding out how young people respond to heavily mediated live performances would make a significant and original contribution to research in drama. The researcher could interview the creators of the work to establish their intention, examine the script and design specifications, examine the design of the mediated elements of the performance and observe the development process, observe the performance and discuss the audience reaction with the young people who attend the performance.

### Using arts-informed research

There has long been a persisting call for teachers to reflect on their own praxis, argued by Friere (1970). Taylor agrees that such research empowers students and teachers to understand and transform their surroundings. While the opportunity for teachers to transform their classrooms is often controlled by contextual factors (Hargreaves and Fullan, 1992), it is also true that teachers who are able to reflect on their own practice can work to shape their development and the learning of their students. In recent research on the professional development of teachers (Anderson, 2002) there is evidence that experienced teachers who can reflect on their situations are better able to change their environment to suit their professional needs.

As practitioners of the arts we have an innate understanding of how arts forms can create and clarify meaning. Although the arts potential in performance, making and appreciating has always been understood, we may not have fully realised the potential of arts research.

Performance ethnography has been suggested as an arts-informed research methodology that can bring about real social change. Norman Denzin (2003) makes a passionate argument for using performance ethnography not only as research but also as a way to influence and change society:

> ... I advance a critical performative pedagogy that turns the ethnographic into the performative and the performative into the political. It is my hope that this pedagogy will allow us to dream our way into a militant democratic utopian space... (2003, pxiii)

Denzin is calling upon researchers to use performance ethnography as praxis for social change, as have Augusto Boal or Dario Fo. This use of arts-informed inquiry rises above research for the social good and works as research for social change. This is radical methodology powered by applied theatrical approaches that Denzin believes can change lives and societies. Denzin identifies and utilises the power of an arts-informed approach. Such approaches move beyond the information abattoir (Carroll, 1996) and introduce the possibility of communicating research in radical ways to achieve lasting change.

Arts informed inquiry could be used as the subject matter and the method of presentation of research in this area. Research findings in the next few years could be presented as a simulation, a piece of machinima[1], a mediated performance or epistemic game. Research is already being presented in these forms but not yet in the arena of drama education, although a new category of research has emerged which investigates the action through the concurrent research into that action: this is practice-based research.

## Practice-based research approaches

A third way in research is wanted that recognises practice as being a central part of research and the reporting of research. Brad Haseman (2006), who has led many of the major debates in drama education, has proposed that we break from the quantitative/qualitative dyad and establish a third way called practice-based or performance research. He says of this approach:

> ... it is possible to argue that a third methodological distinction is emerging. This third category is aligned with many of the values of qualitative research but is nonetheless distinct from it. The principal distinction between this third category and the qualitative and quantitative categories is found in the way

it chooses to express its findings. In this case, while findings are expressed in non-numeric data they present as symbolic forms other than in the words of discursive text. Instead research reporting in this paradigm occurs as rich, presentational forms. ... And so when research findings are made as presentational forms they deploy symbolic data in the material forms of practice; forms of still and moving images; forms of music and sound; forms of live action and digital code. (Haseman, 2006)

When we consider an evolving research field it is difficult to stand back from the practice and observe. Drama educators normally participate in research so no researcher is totally detached. What Haseman is calling for is not dispassionate and detached research but research which is driven directly by the practice it is examining. Rather than beginning with a question, the researcher begins with the practice and seeks to examine it in action and to report on the practice through the practice. This approach, though in its infancy, is especially appropriate for our needs in drama and technology: we are researching the practice as it evolves. By the time we come up with a 'research problem' the technology has become outmoded and new technology has taken its place.

An approach that researches practice allows the researcher to examine and then present the research in performance as a simulation game and as an online process drama with a supporting analytical or exegetical statement to analyse and contextualise the work. In drama and education one can envisage the practice of mediated performance or video or simulation or any other practices spawning excellent research using practice-based methodologies.

## Researching mediated performance – John Carroll
### Exploring the theatre of surveillance

The theatre of surveillance research project of 2001 focused on the growing importance of image consumption in contemporary society caused by the growing use of information technologies in drama and entertainment. The results of this research have been incorporated into the wider discussion of television and mediated performance in Chapter 7.

The research was based on a number of ethnographic performance forms designed to explore the range of surveillance types experienced in our culture and offer an artistic reflection on the process of surveillance as we now experience it. Through a reflexive performance and interview process the research also celebrated the individual's participation in this evolving information-based culture. It also raises the problems of the largely unexamined concepts of persona, role and surveillance that are so much part of the new media culture by looking at the development of television, especially so-called reality shows.

The term 'theatre of surveillance' was coined during the research to cover a range of dramatic techniques that attempted to deal directly with the centrality of electronic image capture and role performance as a primary means of entertainment and identification in contemporary society.

The pressures of globalisation and its accompanying technological changes are evident everywhere in our culture, especially in the arts. As part of this on-going societal change, in the contested space of corporate and public space, electronic surveillance of citizens in all its forms has become a central social institution and critical marker of currently evolving western information societies.

The electronic surveillance of public spaces by video cameras is one aspect of technology now so widespread that it has become a defining characteristic of urban, affluent consumer cultures. With this ongoing cultural shift, wholesale adoption of the technologies of data and image capture is producing new dramatic forms of performance, many of which involve the commodification of personal and private electronic images. The situations are electronically mediated and the images edited to exploit the emotional experience of individuals portrayed within them in ways that are radically different to conventional concepts of role and theatrical performance.

It seems no accident that the recent growth of reality television has dominated our screens. The particularly explicit form embodied in such shows as *Big Brother* has enjoyed huge success around the world. The popularity of the form has been especially strong with young people.

Perhaps the most interesting aspect of the phenomenon is that it has become more popular on the Internet than it was on television. Live video streaming via the Internet has created a huge audience for such shows, the programmes interactively include the audience in the voting to judge, reward or punish individual contestants.

Though called reality television they are not about 'reality' at all (see Chapter 7). They are a product of globalisation and technology and represent the commodification of a new cultural product, the mediated presentation of role performance as 'reality'. This is a new hybrid form of television that takes some elements of documentary but exaggerates and concentrates the focus on emotional conflict. It has evolved a language of its own, borrowed partly from process drama, partly from soap opera, partly from game shows with tabloid packaging and the cinema verité form of film. Through their structure, these programmes promote a view of humanity reduced through endless surveillance to its basic elements, often an individualised win-at-any-cost scramble for money and celebrity. It is a form of economic rationalism edited down to its most elemental form.

## The research project

Based on the theoretical understanding of the centrality of meaning in the consumption of images (Baudrillard, 1998) and Kershaw's (1999) concept of the commodification of performance, the issue of surveillance was explored dramatically through a range of small-scale research productions. They were loosely based on the forms of surveillance used in the security industry. The following list made up the background for the drama and coded the suspicions raised by surveillance into seven types:

- *categorical*: suspicion based on personal characteristics such as dress, race or membership of subculture group
- *transmitted*: surveillance initiated by someone else, eg police, store detective or member of the public
- *behavioural*: suspicion based on behaviour, eg fighting, public display of drunkenness
- *locational*: suspicion based on a person's location, eg walking through a car park notorious for theft late at night
- *personalised*: suspicion based on knowledge of the person surveilled
- *protectional*: suspicion based on fear for personal safety, eg woman at a cash machine late at night
- *voyeuristic*: monitoring based on prurient interest.

(Norris and Armstrong, 1999, p112)

Using categories to produce devised drama performances in this way led to the adoption of a grounded theory methodology in an attempt to engage with the evolving social form and its effect on the audience. The research was aimed at moving from an understanding of audiences as *interpretative communities* of media to a more engaged critical theory stance.

## The research process

In a one-hour session a 23-minute research-devised show was performed for an audience of 60 senior school students. After the performance the audience provided written responses to questions in the programme and participated in seven focus groups of six to eight people. Each group's responses were audiotaped and transcribed.

The live performance consisted of two connected sections, both using video cameras as surveillance devices in the performance. The surveillance categories highlighted in the show were 'categorical' in the first section and 'voyeuristic' in the second. In the first section two young women, obviously students, were shown on video shopping in a mall. The video was projected onto a large screen on the stage and the same performers interacted with the images of themselves. A young male performer with a shopping trolley also interacted with them on the stage. The performances onstage and the video images increasingly deconstructed the nature of the shopping experience and the discipline exerted by the surveillance camera conventions inherent in the shopping mall space itself. The fragmentation of the experience highlighted the levels of surveillance in operation, of which everyday shoppers are unaware. The deconstruction of shopping into its elements of guilt and self-awareness produced responses of recognition from the audience about the surveillance which operates in the mall environment.

This first section of the performance alerted the audiences to the issues of 'categorical suspicion' and established relationships among the performers. In the second section the dramatic scene shifted to a domestic and private moment in the house where the three young people lived. The set was minimally represented on stage through hand props and action. The cameras voyeuristically viewed a bathroom in the house and transmitted the images to a television in a lounge room on the other side of the stage. Another camera projected the image of the audience onto a large screen behind the performers on the stage. A domestic world of relationships was played out on stage, giving the audience the choice of watching two people in a bathroom, a woman watching their behaviour on a television, or watching themselves observing the action.

As the performance developed a more personal, domestic and intimate element in the bathroom scene, the audience was placed in an increasingly voyeuristic position and the pressures of curiosity and embarrassment became more explicit. As one audience member put it:

> I liked the way they brought the audience into it because you were quite happy to watch them go about their lives, until you realised you were back on the screen yourself. Most audiences are more than happy to watch other people in day-to-day life, as long as it's not themselves.

The scene and the tensions within the relationship were explored, a crisis resolved and the performance concluded with the actors watching the audience reaction on a television monitor.

## Results

The written and verbal responses of the audience interviews were open-coded and the results classified as follows:

Surveillance was seen by the audience as

- necessary for social control
- invasive
- open to abuse
- blurring public *versus* private life
- voyeuristic
- a tolerated trade-off for security
- an embarrassment
- a post-modern peepshow.

The performance was seen by the audience as

- helping to understand the issues
- more interesting because of its symbolic form.

Issues of central concern to the audience were

- who controls the watchers?
- technological change and social responsibility.

The strongest theme to emerge in the results from 20 per cent of those interviewed related to the way stage performance provided a form of artistic reflexivity that allowed the audience consciously to consider the issues surrounding surveillance. The next most common response was that surveillance represented a tolerated trade-off for increased levels of personal security. Nevertheless, the audience felt strongly that surveillance was invasive, voyeuristic and that individuals were forced to accept loss of personal space and privacy.

## Conclusions from researching mediated performance

In the new cultural economy, being part of an interpretive community of dramatic and media performers appears no longer sufficient to sustain the cultural connections required for healthy communities. What is required is a reframed dramatic ethnography that allows what Machin and Carrithers (1996) call 'communities of improvisation' to develop. According to Radway (1988) and Ang (1991) *inter alia*, being trapped in the notion that interpretive communities provide a critique of cultural exploitation artificially isolates individuals into categories that may have little relevance to the new social life developing around electronic image reproduction and consumption. Audiences need a space to be able to improvise more freely around the mediated products of culture and experience, especially those involving new forms of media performance.

Live, role-based dramatic performance can provide the shared space necessary for audiences and performers to interact and begin the construction of improvised meaning around issues of surveillance. By contrast, mediated and commodified cultural product, exemplified by reality television, cuts audiences off from any critical interaction with the form despite its attempts at interactivity.

The underlying notion behind the research programme is that new forms of drama need to be designed which are relevant specifically to young audiences. Drama and performance research needs to become part of a community of improvisation that allows a shared conversation to develop which questions the values of the culture. The shift from a modernist to a post-modernist cultural economy in which the circulation of images and information is of central importance; individuals can become 'disembedded' from concrete time and space (Lash and Urry 1994, p13). The proliferation of multiple electronic roles can decentre, destabilise and ultimately diminish the concept of self. From a post-modernist perspective, this can be seen as a celebration of multiple narratives and the fragmentation of outdated certainties.

Whatever position is adopted, the creative artists who provide the social and cultural metacommentary at the heart of drama need to determine how to come to terms with a new media-based culture that celebrates observed performances of 'reality' as acceptable images of the world. Drama needs to find a way to create the communities of improvisation required to sustain a conversation on the issues of persona, identity and role. The theatre of surveillance research project is just one voice that will hopefully add to this conversation in the future.

## Researching video games and other 'trivial' pursuits – David Cameron

I first considered the use of video games as a training tool for my tertiary journalism students in the late 1990s. I had been a video game player for almost three decades and felt no shame about that: games stores were full of middle-aged men with the latest *Xbox* or *PlayStation* magazines tucked under their arms. But I often felt awkward trying to describe how video games could be put to more serious uses, particularly when talking to people who had been teaching since around the time I dropped my first coins into a *Space Invaders* machine.

My initial embarrassment was mostly unfounded. I have generally found many older colleagues genuinely interested and supportive of my work in this area, even when video games remain largely a mystery to their generation. I believe that all good educators are open to new ideas, particularly when they concern the digital generation. After all, the concept of screen-based computer simulation already enjoys a healthy reputation in industries like engineering, aviation, medicine and the military.

As my own research developed, I realised that there was growing interest among educators in the possible applications of video game technology and principles to a greater range of educational and training situations. The last decade has seen a more obvious educational 'movement' (eg Tapscott, 1998; Prensky, 2000, 2006; Gee, 2003; Shaffer, 2005) who argue the case for what has emerged under various titles, such as digital game-based learning, serious gaming, epistemic games or curricular games. Whatever the current title, the field is beginning to define itself in its own terms. It should not be treated simply as the opposite to the entertainment games industry, or as sugar-coated learning. Digital game-based learning is more about taking cognitive and problem-solving systems proven effective in a game situation, and applying them appropriately in wider educational contexts.

The same period has been marked by increased academic interest in the video games themselves. This is driven by a combination of the refinement of the presentation technology into a sophisticated and aesthetically seductive medium, the unique participatory and social aspects afforded by networked gaming technology, and the economic significance of the multi-billion dollar global games industry.

Our children and students are growing up in a world where video games are a significant popular cultural factor. The most publicised research has focused on the possible effects of games on children, such as violence, gender bias, and even the physical effects of prolonged muscle use and eye strain, and how game content should be monitored or controlled. Issues of ratings, pornography, violence, censorship, anti-social behaviour have been considered. These remain heavily contested areas of debate despite 30 years of examination. But academics have now begun to explore more carefully what games are, compared to say movies or live performance, and how we act, react and interact with and through them.

Wider and more rigorous attention is now being given to how video games can and should be studied. For example, can you research a video game unless you have played and understood it yourself? Michael Anderson argued that drama researchers are often a part of the performance being studied: a similar research position confronts many game researchers. These and other interesting questions are being raised, as well as the fundamental issue of where to place games studies in the academy. Is it a science, related to information technology? Does it belong in the humanities, where it can be subject to cross-disciplinary studies such as media studies, literature, drama or psychology in the same way as scholars have approached cinema or television? Some suggest that game studies should be a discipline in its own right, a study of game-play or *ludology* (Frasca, 1999).

There are many reasons why individual teachers, performers and researchers may be interested in video games:

> How do we analyse games? It all depends on who we are, and why we do it. Scholars, gamers, critics and developers all have different needs and need for different methods. As scholars, we may also have different needs and motives, but it might still be possible to come up with common standards. (Aarseth, 2003, p6)

TL Taylor (2005) has suggested that video games can be seen as 'boundary objects' (Star, 1989), in that they provide a common artifact for people with different goals and needs to discuss and analyse. Boundary objects are part of the way in which communities of practice operate and co-operate (see Chapter 1). Just as a printed form in an office can provide shared meaning to different parts of an organisation, video games can provide a common focus for researchers, regardless of their different disciplinary approaches. Taylor also notes that people are not born players of a video game like *EverQuest*: they become players. This process, particularly in large-scale multi-player environments, is similar to the apprenticeships undertaken in other communities of practice. It is important for teachers and performers working in this field to share their stories with a wider audience, to ensure that the communities of practice emerging around games and education continue to develop common ground on which to create new tools, understanding, and creative work. It is equally important that the power of this research, with its ability to capture the image and voice of participants, is handled responsibly.

## Ethical considerations

When we engage in research in drama and theatre education, our first responsibility is to realise that the research process is not a neutral act. Along with the researcher, research studies themselves have power and status because they can interrogate the lived behaviour of students and performers who are the subjects or participants of the research.

Because the politics of research is now a contested area and the social dimensions of the power relationships operating within drama research have become clearer, this asymmetrical power relationship should be considered in terms of outcomes. Who will benefit from the research? Is it only the researcher or can the participants of the research also benefit?

As Foucault (1980) makes clear, power is crucial in the construction of reality. For many drama researchers it is untenable to engage in research that places ultimate control out of the hands of the participants. This becomes more critical when examining research into an area in which the digital native participants have potentially more experience than the digital immigrant researchers in the development of technologically mediated drama. Ownership of the images that emanate from the research is a further complication. If researchers are working with mediated productions, do the research participants own the images? How can anonymity be achieved? How can we provide protection for those whose images are integral to the performance?

A range of discourses has evolved through the exercise of cultural power research which are accepted by our culture as producing truth about the events it participates in and reports on. As Foucault (1980, p33) points out '...everything is dangerous, nothing is innocent'. All situations, especially those involving educational research, reflect some value judgement or ideology on the part of those carrying them out.

However, the alternative power relationships in drama education provide researchers with alternative models. Process drama and Dorothy Heathcote's Commission Model of drama suggest that teachers and learners can share responsibility for the learning. In a similar way there are research models in which researchers and participants have a more equitable distribution of power.

## Conclusion

There are amazing possibilities for research in drama education. So much could be examined that it is difficult to know where to start. Perhaps the best advice for teachers and researchers in drama education who feel bewildered by the choices available is to start with their own practice. There are fine examples of teachers examining how their pedagogies and practices are impacting on those involved in drama learning. Much important research and theory has emerged from these contributions.

This book has provided examples of research in drama and technology education. Much has not yet been touched by formal research but there is a growing tradition of strong research and scholarship in this area which can inform future researchers. There are appropriate and emerging methodologies that fit our field, and resources on arts and drama education research are available or in production.

As practice in drama and technology extends, practitioners will call for research and theory generation to underpin their practice and support new drama educators. The re-shaping of the cultural and pedagogical landscape requires all of us to work in cross-disciplinary ways to uncover the present and future of drama education. The acquired wisdom of drama educators can inform education more broadly if we can find the resources required to probe and liberate knowledge in this exciting field to research the past and imagine the future.

In Chapter 10 we imagine the future of drama education through speculations about learning and draw some conclusions about drama technology and education.

## Note
1 Machinima is the use of video game software to create animated performance. See machinima.com for examples

# 10

## Conclusion:
## Imagining the future

The future is already here. It's just not very evenly distributed yet. (Gibson, 1999)

We don't need a crystal ball to see the future, says science fiction author William Gibson, as the signs are already around us. The problem is that most of us either don't notice or can't make sense of them, which is why we are left wondering 'why didn't I think of that?' as each seemingly obvious but stunningly brilliant innovation comes along.

Soothsaying is a risky business, but we'd like to try to identify some of the signs which point to what the future may hold for the classroom.[1]

Let's start with Lucy.

Lucy is a high school student. She has completed her enrolment using the school's Web-based system. She has paid her school fees online. Looking through some of the information for the subjects she is studying this year, she noticed that they feature online tools like subject wikis, discussion forums, digital game-based learning systems and electronic readings. This morning she attended an information session on how to use the school library's online database of articles and books.

Lucy feels she is well prepared to tackle her senior year of high school. She has a laptop computer that she will use for her assignments and for keeping in touch with her teachers via e-mail. The school provides a wireless network service so she can access the Internet from anywhere on the school grounds. Lucy will be able to use her laptop to research her assignments. She prefers to use the Web to find out new information: she's been planning which university courses to apply for next year in this way, even using the earth-mapping tools of her favourite search engine to compare likely rental costs for accommodation near her preferred campus.

Lucy's computer is also her entertainment system when she's not busy. She's discovered that her public library has a growing collection of movies on DVD. She regularly swaps her favourite audio files with her friends at school. She also has a portable mp3 player that she uses on the bus to and from school and sometimes she downloads podcast study materials recorded by her teachers and made accessible from the school's Website.

Lucy keeps in contact with her friends mainly by using SMS on her mobile phone. Her phone has a built-in still and video camera and she can swap files using a wireless connection to her laptop. She is making a short film for her English class using her phone camera and editing software on her laptop. She can watch her favourite TV shows on her telephone for a small charge, and she can use it to download study guides and sample quizzes for her final exams. She uses online chat at night to talk to her friends while she studies. She regularly receives SMS reminders from school about when assignments are due and where to find study materials online. If she gets stuck on a home-work question, she consults her class blog for tips and examples provided by the teacher.

Lucy is not a real person but a character sketch of a student from the not too distant future, drawn from data gained from surveys of new students and their relationships with technology, plus some straight-out speculation based on emerging technology. The survey sampled 210 first year communication students who were studying journalism, advertising, theatre/media, public relations or commercial radio management majors at Charles Sturt University and first year 280 education students – preservice teachers – at the University of Sydney in 2005. The study found that not only did students use technology constantly; many of them own digital devices.

Not surprisingly mobile telephones have achieved almost complete penetration into this group, as table 10.1 shows. Carroll (2005) identifies the mobile telephone as a key device in the lives of students, for whom interactive technologies are 'entertainment, identity maintenance and communication devices all at the same time'. Students are the core consumers of a reality TV genre that demands audience response via SMS voting.

The ownership of games consoles is interesting, given that most of respondents were young women: 65 per cent of the education group, and 77 per cent

**Table 10.1: Ownership of devices among first-year students**

| Technology | Percentage of ownership | |
|---|---|---|
| | Education | Communication |
| Mobile telephone | 99 | 99 |
| Desktop PC | 80 | 79 |
| Digital still camera | 66 | 49 |
| Game console | 52 | 41 |
| Portable mp3 player | 51 | 30 |

of the communication students. In a world where games are increasingly moving into areas beyond pure entertainment, any shift of gender bias towards game-playing is significant.

The students were asked to self-assess their skill level for a range of online and computer applications and ranked their skills with word processing, e-mail, Web surfing, and instant messaging software as high. Both groups of students recorded only minimal use of high-end video editing software and Web design tools.

**Table 10.2: Students' self-ranking of skills**

| Application | Mean* | |
|---|---|---|
| | Education | Communication |
| Word processing (eg Word) | 4.1 | 4.1 |
| E-mail | 4.3 | 4.0 |
| Web surfing | 4.1 | 3.9 |
| Instant messaging software | 4.0 | 3.8 |
| Digital still camera | 3.1 | 3.7 |
| Presentation software (eg PowerPoint) | 3.2 | 3.4 |
| Spreadsheet (eg Excel) | 3.1 | 3.1 |
| Basic digital video editing (eg iMovie, Movie Maker) | 2.0 | 2.4 |
| Desktop publishing | 3.1 | 2.1 |
| Advanced video editing (eg Final Cut Pro, Premiere) | 1.6 | 1.8 |
| Web design software (eg DreamWeaver) | 1.8 | 1.8 |

* Scale = 1 (do not use), 2 (very unskilled), 3 (unskilled), 4 (skilled), 5 (very skilled)

Instant messaging software is widely used by these students. Research from the Pew Internet and American Life Project indicates a preference among American teenagers towards using instant messaging to communicate with their peers. They use e-mail to talk to 'older people' and institutions or to share complex information with large groups (Lenhart *et al*, 2005, pii).

One of the more obvious trends apparent in our surveys is that students are increasingly reliant on networked digital technology for gathering information and maintaining social relationships (Cameron, 2005). Their use of the Internet as a research tool, and of SMS, e-mail and instant messaging as communication tools, is unlikely to diminish. Their skills and comfort with these tools make them ideal to adapt and utilise in mediated learning situations.

But just because students are comfortable with, or even reliant upon, certain technology doesn't mean they are experts. They use search engines such as Google readily and regularly, giving the appearance of proficient users. But how accurate are they? How good are they at assessing the accuracy or relevance of their search results? Are they aware of the vast amount of information hidden in databases and archives that are not indexed by search engines? There is still plenty of room here for educators to step in and show classes a thing or two about finding, and perhaps more importantly for the Net Generation, critically evaluating information.

## The digital mindset

Step back for a moment to the origins of the generation of students starting university in the first years of the 21st century. Most of them are younger than the first mass-marketed personal computers. Many were born after the Apple Macintosh was launched. Beloit College in Wisconsin (www.beloit.edu) produces an annual list of the 'mindset' factors that separate each generation of first year students from the last cohort, and thus highlights the speed at which evolving technology can become a transparent element of our worldview.

At the time this book was being prepared, we could assume that most of our new students came from a world where:

- computers have always suffered from viruses
- stores have always had scanners at the checkout
- computers have always fitted into their backpacks
- beta is a preview version of software, not a video format
- cyberspace has always existed.

These students live in a world where they have always had a PIN passcode, where fuel has always been unleaded and members of the British royal family have always behaved badly (Beloit College, 2005).

One of the aims of the Beloit mindset lists is to remind staff that each new generation of students presents a unique set of social, historical and cultural reference points. It is a light-hearted but occasionally jarring means of highlighting a perceived generational gap between students and teachers, a gap partly widened by perceptions of and comfort with digital media.

The Beloit mindset lists also show how evolving technology provides shifting cultural signposts for successive generations of students. Johnson (1997, p2) suggests that this has always been part of human experience but that technology used to advance so slowly that it was less easy to see the connections between technological change and other cultural variables. The printing press spread through the modern, post-medieval world over many lifetimes, while the telephone, radio and television spanned a few generations and brought instant changes to society (Gleick, 1999). Computer technology advanced so quickly that Moore's Law described a doubling of processing power every eighteen months, from 2,250 elements in Intel's 1971 microprocessor to 42 million elements in the Pentium 4 chip three decades later (Rheingold, 2003, p58). Think of the speed with which terms like podcast, blog, wiki, and google have entered the educational vernacular.

## The future is participatory

Networked digital environments invite a more active role from the user than most traditional media. At a basic level, this interaction involves clicking on hypertext links on a Web page to navigate through the information. But more powerful applications are rapidly emerging that not only require active engagement to access existing content but invite the user to contribute original content for other people to use.

It is easier for people to make and share a variety of media. Common computer operating systems like Windows or Macintosh OS come loaded up with a range of digital video and imaging tools. The Web abounds with free online tools to create journals (Weblogs or blogs) that can incorporate text, sound and video files. Some people even update their blog using a mobile telephone call (moblogging). Some applications follow a traditional publication model; you can create and publish your own Web page or blog and readers can choose to read or watch or listen to the content.

But some developers have tapped into a do it yourself online media trend to develop tools that rely totally on shared voluntary input from users. For example wiki software, which allows users to create and edit Web pages, has led to the creation of online encyclopaedias (for example Wikipedia) and other tools where the content can come from anyone. There are online tools where people can share photos, comment on and swap favourite Web links, and share lists of their favourite books or films.

One of the possible outcomes of this participatory culture is that students will learn to create works that are not attached to any particular medium. Rather than developing a short classroom live performance as part of a drama lesson, students might develop the original dramatic property and then move on to present it in a range of contexts and media. The technology will allow material to be distributed or performed across different media at the same time. For example, a dramatic property might be presented as a live performance, an edited video-taped performance, a comic book sequence of illustrations, a flash animation, or a downloadable audio file.

The participatory nature of modern media should be seen not as a threat to traditional teaching, but as offering an ideal opportunity to explore ways of presenting dramatic material to different audiences in a range of forms. Similarly, the relative ease with which technology allows a range of production and publishing avenues to be explored simultaneously has implications for learners and teachers working on commissioned projects.

## The future is about communities
Early online technologies such as newsgroups and e-mail lists established a pattern where people of shared interests could 'meet' and discuss even the most obscure interests, regardless of geographical, social or political boundaries in the real world. This has contributed to the growth of online or virtual communities of practice as a key aspect of why we spend time online. Although not everyone will deliberately participate in an obvious community such as an Internet chat group or mailing list, they will inevitably encounter people with shared interests. Their choice of Websites to visit or resources to use will place them in a sub-group of online users that can constitute a community.

At a more advanced level, online communities can be highly organised and committed to their particular concerns or interests. Rheingold (2003) talks about the power of the 'smart mob', a collection of online individuals coordinated to perform a collective action or to solve problems through collective knowledge.

A significant community that already exists is the open source software movement, which licences programmes to be freely shared, modified and enhanced. Some of the most innovative collaborative tools are emerging from this concept that software does not have to be the closed proprietary property of a major company. A range of online tools such as wikis and learning systems such as moodles, are freely distributed on the Web. It is becoming increasingly viable for schools to use this software, rather than paying vast amounts for license fees for proprietary titles.

The refinement of online or virtual communities of practice will be of interest to learners and teachers. Collaborative learning tools and the ability to participate and co-operate in cultural production online will be developed to allow people to learn more effectively.

### The future is always *on*

Ask yourself now – where is your mobile phone? Is it turned on?

In a globally networked environment, concepts such as time zones become irrelevant. Someone, somewhere is awake and producing content. Increasingly, we are permanently interconnected to each other and to media and information sources through our mobile telephones, satellite television services and broadband Internet connections. We are nearly always 'on' as potential media consumers and this will continue as our mobile phones evolve into portable multimedia devices.

Some educators see this as an opportunity for what has been called pervasive learning – using a range of media used beyond the classroom (fax, SMS, posters, mail) to engage the student with learning tasks at anytime, any place. A similar concept has been developed into a gaming phenomenon where a range of technology is used to blur the distinction between the real world and the game world. The *To The Spice Islands* project discussed in Chapter 6 illustrates how everyday technology can be used in this way.

If we are always 'on', we are always potentially 'live'. We have the capacity and the desire to know what is happening now, rather than wait for edited highlights. This also has an impact on the makers of dramatic products for the traditional media. People no longer have to watch television according to the networked schedule: they can buy a whole series on DVD, or download episodes from the Internet. In a world where the distribution model has changed, the provision of live content becomes one of the ways in which media or performance organisations can continue to carve out audiences. Liveness becomes a valuable commodity in itself.

## The future is about trust

People are increasingly relying on trusted sources to help them navigate through and make sense of the enormous volume of information that surrounds us each day. Traditionally, that is what mainstream media organisations have done when creating a newspaper or a radio or TV news bulletin. But we are increasingly deciding for ourselves who to trust, and moving away from the traditional institutions.

Online behaviour has refined this process – think about the types of e-mails you send to and receive from friends. Often our inboxes are full of links to interesting news, jokes, snippets of gossip, or interesting or funny media files. We find something that interests us, we filter through our list of friends and contacts to find people who might share that interest, and we forward the information to them. We are all potentially trusted sources of information for our social networks.

Occasionally we get it wrong. We discover that not everyone on our mailing list is as interested in some topics as we thought they were, or we find our own inbox full of forwarded e-mails from people we don't know all that well. But we can refine our filters and forwarding behaviour and eventually know who to trust, and who will trust us, not to send too many irrelevant or boring e-mails.

Drama education has much to offer students in a world where they are increasingly asked to form their own decisions about which sources of information to trust. Classic drama education exercises revolve around building and earning such trust.

## The future is mobile

In Japan, the word *keitai* has come to mean not only mobile or cell telephones but also the culture surrounding their ownership and use. With some local variations, most cultures share the basics of *keitai*, including an informal etiquette for the use of phones in public spaces and the popularity of text messages for even the most delicate of personal communications.

Mobile telephones are no longer simply about voice communication. They come with text and multi-media message capability, still and video cameras, global positioning satellite (GPS) locators, databases and address books, games and many other software applications. The user interface can be customised to various degrees with downloadable and swappable screensavers, desktop images and ring tones. The telephone hardware itself can be personalised through custom covers or slip-on photograph sleeves.

The more we personalise and customise our mobile telephones, the more integral they become to our daily lives. Many of us now trust important data such as anniversaries, appointments and contact details solely to our telephones. They are always with us and always on. With many western nations reporting mobile phone ownership at more than 100 per cent, we can also assume that they are a truly personal, rather than a shared device.

It is this level of individual ownership, coupled with the increased media capabilities of the devices themselves, that point to a strong future for mobile media technology. Young people are already familiar with forms of media that demand their input via the mobile telephone, such as voting for reality or competition TV programmes. The use of mobile interactivity with television is likely to continue and may well move into other media such as the cinema. Similarly, traditional media such as television and radio are increasingly developing content for delivery on the mobile phone. The mobile phone is an obvious prototype of a personal media/communication device that can handle multiple data input and multimedia content. Precisely because it is technology that is always with us, and that is always on, the mobile telephone is potentially one of the most powerful transformative agents for drama and learning available so far.

At present, *keitai* culture in schools is proscriptive and reactionary. Teachers become frustrated with students who use mobile phones in class and regard it as bad manners or evidence of limited attention span. However, some educators are already looking to a future where students may be requested to turn their telephones on. Prensky (2005, 2006) points out that many mobile phones already carry significant computing power and that appropriate software could easily be developed to turn them into learning and teaching devices. For drama educators looking to blend technology with performance and learning, the mobile telephone is a pervasive and ubiquitous platform beyond the classroom. Prensky (2006, p128) quotes a Japanese student: 'when you lose your mobile, you lose part of your brain'.

### The future is more accessible
In late 2005 the United Nations lent its support to the designers of cheap, hand-cranked laptop computers, designed to use free open source software. One intended group of users is children in developing nations. Throughout this book there has been an assumption that most of its readers live in relatively affluent countries that have technology on tap. The reality is that there are disparities between nations whose citizens have broad access to technology and those who have not, as table 10.3 overleaf illustrates. The

**Figure 10.3: A sample of Internet usage by Country (from Clickz Network, 2006)**

| Nation | Population (CIA World Fact Book) | Internet Users (CIA World Fact Book) | Active Users (Nielsen/ NetRatings) | ISPs (CIA World Fact Book) | Percentage of population Internet Users |
|---|---|---|---|---|---|
| Australia | 20.26 | 14.18 | 10 | 5.4 | 69% |
| Brazil | 188.10 | 25.9 | 12 | 4.4 | 13% |
| Canada | 33.10 | 20.9 | 8.8 | 3.5 | 63% |
| China | 1,310 | 111 | NA | .19 | 8% |
| Jamaica | 2.76 | 1.07 | NA | .0013 | 38% |
| Kenya | 34.70 | 1.5 | NA | .012 | 4% |
| New Zealand | 4.08 | 3.2 | NA | .75 | 78% |
| UK | 60.61 | 37.80 | 24.36 | 4.7 | 62% |
| United States | 298.44 | 203.82 | 143.43 | 195 | 68% |
| Vietnam | 84.40 | 5.87 | NA | .004 | 6% |

*All figures in millions.*

table shows estimates of Internet usage from two sources; the CIA World Fact Book and the Nielsen/NetRatings. Active users are defined as people who go online at least once in a given month.

The reason for this disparity seems straightforward: those with capital are able and willing to invest in more capital and provide opportunities for their citizens through access and education relating to technologies, whereas millions of people have more pressing, fundamental human concerns than to worry about the consumer technologies. Some nations are concerned about the political and cultural implications of giving citizens wide access to networked technology and information media.

Discussion around closing the divide is interesting. In a study developed for the World Bank, Dasgupta, Lall and Wheeler (2000, p15) suggest that there are immediate ways to narrow the divide:

> Our results show that income differentials matter, but they also highlight the critical role of progressive policies. Policy simulations based on our results suggest that feasible reforms could sharply narrow the digital divide during the next decade for many countries in Africa, Asia and Latin America. Our review of the literature also suggests that access promotion would yield substantial benefits for poor households, and that cost effective intervention strategies are available.

We have observed street children in cities from Hanoi to Mumbai, even in the poorer neighbourhoods, using Internet cafes for chat and gaming. The emergence of a technology and media economy in India also suggests that the divide is changing. So the raw figures may not tell the whole story. This digital divide is also a reality for many communities in first world countries.

The digital divide is an important consideration in observing the ways in which information and ideas are controlled in societies around the world. Some see the borderless world of the Internet and cyberspace as a means of bypassing the traditional gatekeepers of information, such as censorial governments, news editors, and public relations spin doctors. Media magnate Rupert Murdoch (2005) observed that younger people in industrialised societies will expect to access a range of information and news sources:

> I'm a digital immigrant. I wasn't weaned on the Web, nor coddled on a computer. Instead, I grew up in a highly centralised world where news and information were tightly controlled by a few editors, who deemed to tell us what we could and should know. My two young daughters, on the other hand, will be digital natives. They'll never know a world without ubiquitous broadband Internet access.

This book is about the potential for technology to assist in providing positive learning and performance experiences. Part of this approach includes access to communities of practice that can provide specialist knowledge to assist students realise the learning potential afforded by situated role, live engagement in the process, and simulated or real learning commissions.

The digital divide is often perceived as the dark cloud in technology's silver lining. We believe that drama educators can humanise technology by showing that the most important interface with other people is through human interaction. Although this can be mediated through a computer, human to human interaction has always been and will always be the most effective way to communicate.

Drama is particularly well placed as a curriculum element which can enable schools to cope with changing technology, the media content that comes with it and the cultural changes that result. Drama has always provided tools to understand and explore the issues and potentials of change. As Dorothy Heathcote has noted, drama is an eternal 'shape-shifter' in the real world, able to adapt to and harness 'close encounters' with other cultural forces. Technology allows similar dynamic relationships in the virtual worlds of networked communication, mediated performance and video games.

Drama's ability to experiment safely with new thoughts and ways of doing things is valuable. Playful production in the classroom can push beyond the boundaries of the real into virtual and imaginary worlds.

This book started with a journey back in time, to the wreck of the Dutch trading ship *Batavia* in 1629. With the benefit of historical hindsight, the conventions of process drama, the creative power of available media technologies and the imagination of students and teachers, building a time machine was a simple affair compared with forecasting the future directions of drama, education and technology.

Perhaps, as technologist Alan Kay suggests, 'the best way to predict the future is to invent it' (Prensky, 2001a, p38).

## Notes

1 Some of the themes presented in this chapter were inspired by *The Future of Media* event held in Melbourne, Australia in November 2005. In the absence of material to cite formally, we would like to acknowledge in particular the ideas and discussions generated by Dale Peskin, Sophie Walpole, Mark Pesce, John Wyver, Peter Giles, Rob Antulov, Geoff Lowe, Angela Beasley, and Rachel Dixon.

# References

Aarseth, E (1997) *Cybertext, Perspectives on Ergodic Literature.* Baltimore: Johns Hopkins University Press

Aarseth, E (2003) 'Playing Research: Methodological Approaches to Game Analysis', *DAC2003*, Melbourne, retrieved 10 November 2004, from http://hypertext.rmit.edu.au/dac/papers/Aarseth.pdf

Abbs, P (ed) (1987) *Living Powers: The Arts in Education*, London: Falmer

Ackroyd, J (2000) 'Applied Theatre: Problems and Possibilities', Applied Theatre Journal, (1), retrieved 10 April 2006, from http://www.griffith.edu.au/centre/cpci/atr/journal/article1_number1.htm

Adams, D (2001) 'So Long, Douglas Adams, and Thanks for All the Fun', http://dir.salon.com/story/tech/feature/2001/05/15/douglas_adams/index.html

Anderson, M (2002) Journeys in Teacher Professional Development, [unpublished doctoral thesis], Sydney: The University of Sydney

Anderson, M (2004) 'Drama Futures: Possibilities for Research, Advocacy and Policy in the 21st Century', NJ: *The National Journal of Drama Australia*, 28(2), pp31-41

Anderson, M (2005) 'New Stages: Challenges for Teaching the Aesthetics of Drama Online', *Journal of Aesthetic Education*, 39(2), pp2-12

Ang, I (1991) *Desperately Seeking the Audience*, London: Routledge

Arena Theatre Company, (2005) *Company Statement.* Retrieved 10 November, 2005 from http://www.arenatheatre.com.au/aboutarena/companystatement.html

Arts Education Partnership (2004) *The Arts and Education: New Opportunities for Research*, Washington: Arts Education Partnership

Auslander, P (1999) *Liveness: Performance in a Mediatized Culture*, London: Routledge

Auslander, P (2002) 'Live from Cyberspace: Or, I Was Sitting at My Computer This Guy Appeared He Thought I Was a Bot', *Performing Arts Journal*, 70, pp16-21

Australian Bureau of Statistics (2002) 'Attendance at Selected Cultural Venues and Events, Australia, 2002', retrieved 10 November 2005, from http://www.abs.gov.au/Ausstats/abs@.nsf/0/39BCCBB0187DF4A5CA256DCD0081889A

Australian Bureau of Statistics (2004) 'Household Use of Technology', retrieved 10 November 2004 from http://www.abs.gov.au/Ausstats/abs@.nsf/Lookup/F4C72A98CCAB42EDCA2568A900143AB5

Australian/Netherlands Maritime Research Centre (2003) 'To the Spice Islands', retrieved 12 June, 2005 from http://www.csu.edu.au/newmedia/batavia/

Bainbridge, J (2004) 'Teens Love Interactive Media', in Yahoo and Carat Interactive study, 'Born to be Wired', *B and T Weekly*, April, 54(2), p25

Banham, M (ed) (1988) *The Cambridge Guide to World Theatre*, Cambridge: Cambridge University Press

Barnes, S (2001) *Online Connections: Internet Interpersonal Relationships*, New Jersey: Hampton Press Inc

Bateson, G (1972) *Steps to Ecology of Mind*, New York: Ballantine Books

Baudrillard, J (1994) *Simulacra and Simulation, Selected Writings*, ed. Mark Poster Stanford; Stanford University Press, 1988, pp.166-184.

Baudrillard, J (1998) *The Consumer Society: Myths and Structures*, Thousand Oaks, CA: Sage Publications

Beck, U (1992) *Risk society: Towards a New Modernity*, London: Sage

Bell, D (2001) *An Introduction to Cybercultures*, London: Routledge

Beloit College, (2005) 'Beloit College Mindset Lists', *Beloit College*, retrieved 11 April, 2005, from http://www.beloit.edu/%&Epubaff/mindset/

Benjamin, W (1969) *Illuminations*, New York: Schocken [Also available at http://bid. berkeley.edu/bidclass/readings/benjamin.html]

Benjamin, W (1973) 'Program for a Proletarian Children's Theatre', translated by Susan Buck-Morss, *Performance* 1(5), p31

Blast Theory, (2004) retrieved 10 April 2005, fromhttp://www.blasttheory.co.uk/bt/about. html

Boal, A (1979) *Theatre of the Oppressed*, London: Pluto Press

Boal, A (1995) *The Rainbow of Desire: The Boal Method of Theatre and Therapy*, New York: Routledge

Board of Studies, (2003) *Drama: Years 7-10 Syllabus*, Sydney: Board of Studies New South Wales

Bolton, G (1993) 'Drama in Education and TIE: a Comparison', in T Jackson (ed) *Learning Through Theatre: New Perspectives on Theatre in Education*, London: Routledge

Bolton, G (1996) 'Afterword: Drama as Research', in P Taylor (ed) *Researching Drama and Arts Education*, London: Falmer Press

Bolton, G (1998) *Acting in Classroom Drama: A Critical Analysis,* Stoke on Trent: Trentham Books

Bolter, JD and Grusin, D (1999) *Remediation: Understanding New Media*, Cambridge: MIT Press

Bowell, P and Heap, B (2002) *Planning Process Drama*, London: David Fulton

Brook, P (1980) *The Empty Space*, Harmondsworth: Penguin

Brunton, C (2004) *Youth Audience Research: Motivations and Barriers to Attendance Amongst 12-17 Year Olds,* Melbourne: Arts Victoria

Bush, N (2001) *Artificial Intelligence Markup Language (AIML) Version 1.0.1.* retrieved 10 April 2006, from http://alicebot.org/TR/2001/WD-aiml

Cameron, D (2005) *The Net Generation goes to University?*, Proceedings of the Journalism Education Association conference, Surfers Paradise, retrieved 12 December 2005, from http://live-wirez.gu.edu.au/jea.papers/CAMERON.RTF

Cameron, D and Carroll, J (2004) 'The Story So Far... The Researcher as a Player in Games Analysis', *Media International Australia: Games and Gaming*, February, 1, p 68

Carroll, J (1982) 'Growing Language', *National Association for Drama in Education Journal*, 7(2), pp59-62

Carroll, J (1986) 'Framing Drama: Some Classroom Strategies', *National Association for Drama in Education Journal*, 10(2), pp 5-7

Carroll, J (1988) 'Terra Incognita: Mapping drama talk', *National Association for Drama in Education Journal*, 12(2), pp 13-21

Carroll, J (2002a) 'The Theatre of Surveillance: Invisible Theatre for Invisible Audiences', in B Rasmussen and A-L Ostern (eds) *Playing Betwixt and Between: The Idea Dialogues 2001*, Bergen: IDEA, pp 203-208

Carroll, J (2002b) 'Digital drama: A Snapshot of Evolving Forms', *Drama and Learning: Melbourne Studies in Education*, November, 43(2), pp130-141

Carroll, J (2004a) 'Digital Interactive Drama and process Drama', *Drama Research*, 3, Gateshead, UK: National Drama publications, pp 89-99

Carroll, J (2004) 'Digital Pre-text: Process Drama and Everyday Technology' in C Hattton and M Anderson, *State of Our Art: NSW Perspectives in Educational Drama*, Sydney: Currency Press, pp66-77

Carroll, J (2005a) 'Digital Natives and Virtual Literacy: Process Drama and On-line Learning', *International Journal of Learning*, 11, Havana, Cuba: Proceedings of The Eleventh International Literacy and Education Research Network Conference, 2004, pp1211-1217

Carroll, J (2005b) 'YTLKIN2ME? Drama in the Age of Digital Reproduction', NJ *Drama Australia Journal*, 29(1) and *IDEA Journal*, 3, pp15-23

Carroll, J and Cameron, D (2003) *To the Spice Islands: Interactive Process Drama*, proceedings of the DAC conference 2003, published by the Fine Art Forum, retrieved 10-4-06 hypertext.rmit.edu.au/dac/papers/Carroll.pdf

Carroll, J and Cameron, D (2005) 'Playing the Game: Role Distance and Digital Performance', *IDEA/Applied Theatre Research Journal*, 6

Carroll, J, Howard, S, Peck, J and Murphy, J (2002) 'A field study of perceptions and use of mobile telephones by 16 to 22 year olds, *Journal of Information Technology Theory and Application*, 4(2), pp49-62

Cheung, C (2000) 'A Home on the Web: Presentations of the Self on Personal Home Pages', D Gauntlett (ed) *Web.studies: Rewriting Media Studies for the Digital Age*, London: Arnold

Clickz Network (2006) Population explosion!, retrieved 16 April 2006 from http://www.clickz.com/stats/sectors/geographics/article.php/5911_151151

Coleridge, ST (1907) *Biographia Literaria*, Vol 2, J Shawcross (ed), Oxford, Clarendon Press

Contact Youth Theatre (2004) *Annual Review 2003-2004*. Contact Youth Theatre. Manchester

Cuban, L (1986) *Teachers and Machines: The Classroom Use of Technology Since 1920*, New York: Teachers College Press

Cuban, L (2001) *Oversold and Underused: Computers in the Classroom*, Cambridge: Harvard University Press

Danet, B (2001) *Cyberplay: Communication Online*, Berg: Oxford

Dasgupta, S, Lall, S and Wheeler, D (2000) *Policy Reform, Economic Growth, and the Digital Divide: An Econometric Analysis*, retrieved 10 April 2006, from http://econ.worldbank.org/files/1615 wps2567.pdf

Dash, M (2002) *Batavia's Graveyard: The True Story of the Mad Heretic Who Led History's Bloodiest Mutiny*, New York: Three Rivers Press de Marinis, M (1987) The Dramaturgy of the Spectator, quoted in B Kershaw (1999) *The Radical in Performance*, London: Routledge

Denzin, NK (2003) *Performance Ethnography: Critical Pedagogy and the Politics of Culture*, Thousand Oaks, CA: Sage Publications

Deshler, D and Selener, D (1991) 'Transformative Research: In Search of a Definition', *Convergence*, XXIV(3), p9

Dienst, R (1994) *Still Life in Real Time: Theory After Television*, NC: Duke University Press

Eco, U (1989) *The Open Work*, translated by A Cancogni, Cambridge: Harvard University Press

Erikson, E (1968) *Identity, Youth and Crisis*, New York: Norton

Eskelinen, M (2001) 'The Gaming Situation', *The International Journal of Computer Games Research*, July, 1(1), retrieved 10 April 2006 from http://www.gamestudies.org/0101/eskelinen/

Featherstone, M (1991) *Consumer Culture and Postmodernism*, London: Sage

Flew, T (2002) *New Media: An Introduction*, South Melbourne: Oxford

Flintoff, K (2002a) Of Bodies in Place or In Place of Bodies in Rasmussen, B and A Ostern (eds) *Playing Betwixt and Between*, Bergen: IDEA Publications

Flintoff, K (2002b) Interfacing: Drama, The Arts and ICT. Unpublished article

Foster, P (2002) 'Using Case-Study Analysis in Technology Education Research', *Journal of Career and Technical Education*, Fall, 19(1), pp32-46

Foucault, M (1980) 'Truth and Power' in C Gordon (ed) *Power/Knowledge: Selected Interviews and Other Writings, 1972-1977*, New York: Pantheon Books

Foucault, M (1986) 'On the Genealogy of Ethics: an Overview of Work in Progress', in Paul Rabinow *The Foucault Reader*, Harmondsworth: Penguin

Frasca, G (1999) 'Ludology Meets Narratology: Similitudes and Differences Between (Video) Games and Narrative', retrieved 30 November 1999, from http://www.ludology.org [originally published in Finnish as (1999) 'Ludologia Kohtaa Narratologian', *Parnasso*, 3]

Friere, P (1970) *The Pedagogy of the Oppressed*, Houndsworth: Penguin

Friere, P (1985) *The Politics of Education: Culture, Power and Liberation*, translated by Donaldo Macedo, South Hadley: Bergin and Garvey

Fromme, J (2001) *Computer Games as a Part of Children's Culture*, retrieved July 2003, from http://www.gamestudies.org/0301/fromme/

Fry, T (1993) *R U A TV: Heidegger and the Televisual*, T Fry (ed), Sydney: Power Publications, Introduction

Gee, J (2005) 'What Would a State of the Art Instructional Video Game Look Like?', *Innovate*, 1(6), para5

Gee, JP (2003) *What Video Games Have to Teach Us About Learning and Literacy*, New York: Palgrave

Gibson, W (1999) *NPR Talk of the Nation*, retrieved 30 November 1999, from http://discover.npr.org/features/feature.jhtml?wfId=1067220

Giddens, A (1991) *Modernity and Self-Identity*, Cambridge: Polity Press

Gleick, J (1999) *Faster: The Acceleration of Just About Everything*, New York: Pantheon

Goffman, E (1974) *Frame Analysis*, Norwich: Peregrine

Goffman, E (1990) *The Presentation of Self in Everyday Life*, Harmondsworth: Penguin

Goleman, D (1995) *Emotional Intelligence*, London: Bloomsbury Publishing

Green, B, Reid, J and Bigum, C (1998) 'Teaching the Nintendo Generation? Children, Computer Culture and Popular Technologies', in S Howard (ed) *Wired-up: Young People and the Electronic Media*, London: UCL Press

Green, C and Bigum, B (1993) 'Aliens in the Classroom', *Australian Journal of Education*, 37, pp119-141

Hall, S (2000) 'Who Needs 'Identity'?' in du Gay, J Evans and P Redman (eds) *Identity: A Reader*, London: Sage

Hargreaves, A. and Fullan, M. (1992) Introduction. In Hargreaves, A. and M. Fullan (Eds), *Understanding Teacher Development* (pp 1-19) Columbia, Teachers College Press.

Harju, H (1997) *Philip Auslander: Reimagining the Project of Political Art*, retrieved 12 September 2005, from, http://www.teak.fi/teak/ACT/auslander.html

Hartfield, G (1982) Workbook of Sociology, Stuttgart: Kroener

Haseman, B (1991) 'Improvisation, Process Drama and Dramatic Art', *The Journal of National Drama*, July 1991, pp19-21

Haseman, B (2004) 'Cooking and Drama Education in the Global Kitchen', NJ: Drama Australia Journal, 28(2), pp15-25

Haseman, B (2006) 'A Manifesto for Performative Research', *Media Information Australia* No.118, pp 98-106

Heathcote, D (1969) 'Dramatic Activity', *Drama, English in Education*, 3(2)

Heathcote, D (1984) *Drama and Social Change* [lecture series], Kohia Teachers Centre

Heathcote, D (1991) *Collected Writings on Education and Drama*, Evanston, Ill: Northwestern University Press

Heathcote, D (1993) 'Drama as Radical Pedagogy: Agency and Power in the Classroom', [Interview with J Carroll], *Teaching Education Journal*, 9(1)

Heathcote, D (2003) 'A Vision Possible: The Commission Model of Teaching', *Drama*, 11(1), pp16-27

Hertzberg, M (2003) 'Engaging Critical Reader Response to Literature Through Process Drama', *Reading Online*, 6(10), retrieved 10 April 2006, from http://www.reading online.org/international/inter_index.asp?HREF=hertzberg/http://dir.salon.com/tech/fe atures/2001/05/15/

Humphrys, J (2000) *The Devil's Advocate*, London: Arrow

Jackson, A (1999) 'The Centrality of the Aesthetic in Educational Theatre', *NJ Drama Australia Journal*, 23(2), pp51-64

Johnson, S (1997) *Interface Culture: How New Technology Transforms the Way We Create and Communicate*, San Franscisco, Harper

Jackson, T (ed) (1993) *Learning Through Theatre: New Perspectives on Theatre in Education*, London, Routledge

Johnson, S (2005) *Everything Bad is Good for You*, London, Penguin

Jordan, N (2002) 'How New is New Media? The History of Multi-Media Usage in Theatrical Productions', *NJ: Drama Australia Journal*, 26(2) pp73-82

Katz, J (2000) *Up, Up, Down, Down*, retrieved 26 September 2001, from http://www. slashdot.org/features/00/11/27/1648231.shtml

Kelso, M, Weyhrauch, TP and Bates, J (1993) Dramatic Presence in Presence: Teleoperators and virtual environments, *MIT Journal* Vol 2 No1 pp1-15

Kershaw, B (1999) *The Radical in Performance*, London: Routledge

Knezek, G and Christensen, R (2002) 'Impact of New Information Technologies on Teachers and Students', *Education and Information Technologies*, 7(4)

Kolb, B (1997) 'Pricing as the Key to Attracting Students to the Performing Arts', *Journal of Cultural Economics*, 21, pp139-146

Kotler, P and Sheff, J (1996) *Standing Room Only: Strategies for Marketing the Performing Arts*, Cambridge: Harvard Business School Press

Kress, G (2003) *Literacy in the New Media Age*, London: Routledge

LaFarge, A (1995) 'A World Exhilarating and Wrong: Theatrical improvisation on the Internet', *Leonardo*, 28, pp415-422

Lanham, R (1993) *The Electronic Word: Democracy, Technology, and the Arts*, Chicago: Chicago University Press

Lankshear, C Snyder, I and Green, B (2000) *Teachers and Technoliteracy: Managing Literacy, Technology and Learning in Schools*, Sydney: Allen and Unwin

Lash, S and Urry, J (1994) *Economies of Signs and Spaces*, London: Sage

Lather, P (1992) 'Critical Frames in Educational Research: Feminist and Post-Structuralist Perspectives', *Theory Into Practice*, XXXI(2), p87

Laurel, B (1991) *Computers as Theatre*, Menlo Park, CA: Addison Wesley

Lave, J and Wenger, E (1991) *Situated Learning: Legitimate Peripheral Participation*, Cambridge: Cambridge University Press

Leedy, P and Ormrod, J (2001) *Practical Research, Planning and Design*, Columbus, Ohio: Merrill Prentice Hall

Lenhartz, A, Madden, M and Hitlin, P (2005) 'Teens and Technology. Pew Internet and American Life Project', retrieved 12 September 2005, from http://www.pewinternet.org

Leyland, B (1996) How Can Computer Games Offer Deep Learning and Still Be Fun? A Progress Report on a Game in Development [paper delivered at ASCILITE conference, Adelaide, 2-4 December 1996], retrieved 9 July 2003, from http://www.ascilite.org.au/conferences/adelaide96/papers/14.html

Machin, D and Carrithers, M (1996) 'From 'interpretative communities' to 'communities of improvisation", *Media, Culture and Society*, 18, 343-352

Manovich, L (1999) 'What is Digital Cinema?' in P Lunenfeld (ed) *The Digital Dialectic: New Essays on New Media*, Cambridge: MIT Press

Mateas, M (2004) 'A Preliminary Poetics for Interactive Drama and Games', in N Wardrip-Fruin and P Harrigan (eds) *First person New Media and Story, Performance, and Game*, Cambridge: The MIT Press

McGonigal, J (2003) "This is Not a Game': Immersive Aesthetics and Collective Play', *Proceedings of the 5th International Digital Arts and Culture conference*, Melbourne

McGrath, J (2004) *Loving Big Brother*, London: Routledge, p167

McLean, J (1996) 'An Aesthetic Framework in Drama: Issues and Implications', *NADIE Research Monograph Series*, Brisbane: NADIE, 2

Mooney, M (2004) 'Morphing Into Screen Drama', in Hatton and M Anderson (eds) *The State of Our Art: NSW Perspectives in Educational Drama*, Sydney: Currency Press and Educational Drama Association of New South Wales, pp 90-103

Morris, A (2004) Technology in the Drama Classroom, in M Mooney and J Nicholls (eds) *Drama Journeys: Inside Drama Learning*, Strawberry Hills: Currency Press, pp 133-148

Murdoch, R (2005) 'Speech by Rupert Murdoch to the American Society of Newspaper Editors, April 13, 2005', retrieved 12 September 2005, from http://www.newscorp.com/news/news_247.html

Murphy, S (2003) *Metro*, 30 May, p17

Murray, J (1997) *Hamlet on the Holodeck: the Future of Narrative in Cyberspace*, New York: The Free Press

Myers, R (2005) Interview with Michael Anderson on 24 October 2005

Nakamura, L (2000) 'Race in/for Cyberspace: Identity Tourism and Racial Passing on the Internet', in D Bell and B. Kennedy (eds) *The Cybercultures Reader*, London: Routledge

National Endowment for Science, Technology and the Arts, *Awardee Story: John McGrath*, retrieved 10th April 2006, from http://www.nesta.org.uk/ourawardees/profiles/5021/index.html

National Institute of Dramatic Art (1998) *StageStruck*, CD Rom Copyright:NIDA

National Statistics (2004) Attendance at cultural events: Social Trends 34, retrieved 12 November 2005, from http://www.statistics.gov.uk/STATBASE/ssdataset.asp?vlnk=7188

Neelands, J (2004). 'Miracles are Happening: Beyond the Rhetoric of Transformation in the Western Traditions of Drama Education', *Research in Drama Education*, 9(1), pp47-56

Neelands, J and Goode, T (2000) *Structuring Drama Work: A Handbook of Available Forms in Theatre and Drama, 2nd edn*, Cambridge: Cambridge University Press

Nicholson, H (2005) *Applied Drama: The Gift of Theatre*, UK: Palgrave

Norris, C and Armstrong, G (1999) *The maximum surveillance society: the rise of CCTV*, Oxford: Berg Pubslishers

O'Neill, C (1988) 'The Nature of Dramatic Action', NADIE Journal – Journal of Drama Australia, 12(2)

O'Neill, C (1995) *Drama worlds: A Framework for Process Drama*, Portsmouth: Heinemann

O'Toole, J and Bundy, P (1993) 'Kites and Magpies: TIE in Australia', in T Jackson (ed), *Learning Through Theatre: New Perspectives on Theatre in Education*, London, Rutledge. pp133-150

O'Toole, J (1998) 'Playing on the Beach. Consensus among Drama Teachers – Some Patterns in the Sand', *National Association for Drama Education Journal*, 22(2), pp5-19

Oblinger, D and Oblinger, J (2005) 'Educating the Net generation', *Educause*, retrieved September 2005, from http://www.educause.edu/educatingthenetgen/

Office for Standards in Education (2004) 'Inspecting English and Drama', retrieved 10th November 2004, from http://www.ofsted.gov.uk/inspectors/docs/conferences/english_inspdrama.pdf

Patching, R (2002) 'Work Experience at Major Events: Is it Worth the Bother?' *Asia Pacific Media Educator*, 11, pp129-140

Perlin, K (2004) 'Can There be a Form between a Game and a Story?', in N Wardrip-Fruin and P Harrigan (eds) *First Person: New Media as Story, Performance, and Game*, Cambridge: MIT Press

Poole, S (2000) *Trigger Happy: Videogames and the Entertainment Revolution*, New York: Arcade

Powell, C (1996) 'Interview with Jaron Lanier', *Scientific American.com*, retrieved 12 November 2005, from http://www.sciam.com/article.cfm?articleID=00070110-E9C1-1CD9-B4A8809EC588EEDF&pageNumber=2&catID=4

Prensky, M (2001a) Digital Game-Based Learning, New York: McGraw-Hill

Prensky, M (2001b) 'Digital natives, Digital immigrants', *On the Horizon*, 9(5)

Prensky, M (2005) 'What Can You Learn From a Cell Phone? Almost Anything!', *Innovate* 1(5), retrieved 26 January 2006, from http://www.innovateonline.info/index.php?view=article&id=83

175

Prensky, M (2006) *'Don't bother me mom – I'm learning'*: St Paul, Minnesota, Paragon House

Radway, J (1988) *Reading the Romance: Women, Patriarchy, and Popular Literature*, Chapel Hill, University of North Carolina Press

Rasmussen, B (2002) *'Playing Betwixt and Between: The IDEA Dialogues 2001'*, Bergen, Norway: IDEA Publications

Readman, K and Wise, J (2004) 'Aesthetic Pedagogy and Digital Resource Design: Some Considerations', *Change: Transformations in Education*, 7(2), November, pp89-104

Rheingold, H (2003) *Smart Mobs: The Next Social Revolution*, Cambridge, MA: Perseus

Rheingold, H (2004) *Background Briefing*, ABC Radio National, Australia, retrieved April 25, 2004, from http://www.abc.net.au/rn/talks/bbing/

Ryan, ML (1997) 'Interactive Drama: Narrativity in a Highly Interactive Environment', *MFS Modern Fiction Studies*, 43(3), pp677-707

Ryan, ML (2001) *Narrative as Virtual Reality*, Baltimore: John Hopkins University Press

Sarantakos, S (1993) *Social Research*, Melbourne: Macmillan

Shaffer, DW (2004) Epistemic frames for epistemic games, *Computers and Education*, 46, pp 223 – 234.

Shaffer, DW (2005) Epistemic games, *Innovate*, 1 (6), retrieved 15 April, 2005, from http://www.innovate.info/index.php?view=article&id=79

Shaffer, DW and Resnick, M (1999) 'Thick Authenticity: New Media and Authentic Learning', *Journal of Interactive Learning Research*, 10(2), pp195-215

Shaffer, DW and Gee, J (2005) 'Before Every Child is Left Behind: How Epistemic Games Can Solve the Coming Crisis in Education', *WCER* Working Paper, 2005-7, Wisconsin Center for Education Research, p24

Shaffer, DW, Squire, K, Halverson, R and Gee JP (2005) *Video Games and The Future of Learning*, WCER Working Paper, 2005-4, Wisconsin Center for Education Research

Shaughnessy, N (2005) 'Truths and Lies: Exploring the Ethics of Performance Applications', *Research in Drama Education*, June 10(2), pp201-212

Shepherd, C (2001) 'Games E-learners Play', retrieved 18 November 2005, from http://www.fastrak-consulting.co.uk/tactix/Features/games.htm

Smith, R, Curtin, P and Newman, L (1997) 'Kids in the Kitchen: The Educational Implications of Computers and Computer Games Used by Young Children', retrieved 9 July 2003, from http://www.fed.qut.edu.au/crn/resource/aera.html

Squire, K and Jenkins, H (2004) 'Harnessing the Power of Games in Education', *Insight*, 3(1), p5-33

Stake, R (1995) *The Art of Case Study Research*, Thousand Oaks, California: Sage Publications

Star, SL and Griesemer, JR (1989) 'Institutional Ecology, 'Translations' and Boundary Objects: Amateurs and Professionals in Berkeley's Museum of Vertebrate Zoology, 1907-39', *Social Studies of Science*, 19(3), pp387-420

Stoker, B (1974) *Dracula*, London: Arrow Books

Strauss, W and Howe, N (1997) *The Fourth Turning*, New York: Broadway

Sutton, P (2004) 'Face facts'. The Livingnewspaper.com website, retrieved 12 August 2005, from http://www.thelivingnewspaper.com/

Sutton, P and Shaughnessy, N (2002) Tomorrow's Front Pages, Unpublished paper presented for the IFTR (International Federation for Theatre Research), Amsterdam, July

Swortzell, L (1993) 'Trying to Like TIE', in T Jackson *Learning through Theatre: New Perspectives on Theatre in Education*, London: Routledge, pp133-149

Tapscott, D (1998) *Growing Up Digital: The Rise of the Net Generation*, New York: McGraw-Hill

Taylor, P (1995) 'Pre-text and Storydrama: The Artistry of Cecily O'Neill and David Booth', *NADIE Research Monograph* 1, Brisbane, p13

Taylor, P (ed) (1996) *Researching Drama and Arts Education*, London: Falmer Press.

Taylor, P (1998) *Redcoats and Patriots: Reflective Practice in Drama and Social Studies*, Portsmouth, NH: Heinemann

Taylor, TL (2005) Contemporary Play: How MMOGs Can Inform Game Studies, keynote paper presented at DiGRA conference, Vancouver, Canada.

Tulloch, J (2000) *Watching Television Audiences: Cultural Theories and Methods*, London: Arnold

Turkle, S (1997) *Life on the Screen: Identity in the Age of the Internet*, New York: Touchstone

Turner, V (1983) 'Liminal to Liminoid, in Play, Flow, and Ritual: An Essay in Comparative Symbology', in JC Harris and RJ Park (eds) *Play, Games and Sports in Cultural Contexts*, Champaign, Il: Human Kinetics Publishers Inc

Virilio, P (1989) *War and Cinema: The Logistics of Perception*, translated by Patrick Camille, London: Verso

Wallace, RS (2002) PNAMBIC, retrieved 16 April 2006, from http://alicebot.org/articles/wallace/pnambic.html

Wardrip-Fruin, N and Harrigan, P (2004) 'Introduction to Cyberdrama', in N Wardrip-Fruin and P Harrigan, *First Person: New Media as Story, Performance, and Game*, Cambridge: The MIT Press

Weeks, J (1995) *Invented Moralities: Sex Values in an Age of Uncertainty*, Cambridge: Polity Press

Wenger, E (1998) 'Communities of Practice: Learning as a Social System', *Systems Thinker*, retrieved 7 August, 2005, from http://www.co-i-l.com/coil/knowledge-garden/cop/lss.shtml

Westwood, S (1992) 'Power Knowledge: The Politics of Transformative Research', *Studies in the Education of Adults*, 24(2), pp191- 198

Williams R (1990) *Television: Technology and Cultural Form*, 2nd ed, London: Routledge

Witkin, RW (1974) *The Intelligence of Feeling*, London: Heinemann

Wright, R, Hedberg, JG and Harper, B (1998) 'Learner Construction of Knowledge: Using StageStruck to Develop a Performance', in R Corderoy (ed) *Flexibility: The Next Wave*, [Proceedings of the 15th Annual Conference of the Australasian Society for Computers in Learning in Tertiary Education, 14-16 December], Wollongong, NSW: University of Wollongong, pp. 673-679, retrieved 2 July 2005, from http://www.ascilite.org.au/conferences/wollongong98/asc98-pdf/wrighthedbergharper0165.pdf

Wyver, J, (1999) Foreword in *Desert Rain: A virtual Game/Installation*. Blast Theory, London.

Zipes, J (1973) 'Building a Children's Theatre: Two documents', *Performance*, 1(5), pp22-24

# Index